Life is Hard
God is Good
Let's Dance

Life is Hard
God is Good
Let's Dance

Experiencing Real Joy in a World Gone Mad

Brant Hansen

Bestselling author of *Unoffendable*

W Publishing Group

AN IMPRINT OF THOMAS NELSON

This book is dedicated to my mom, Linda.
We went through a lot, didn't we?

In the world you will have tribulation;
but be of good cheer,
I have overcome the world.

—Jesus[1]

Contents

One Weird Kid

There's a meme that's a photo of a golden retriever in a helicopter pilot's seat, with a headset on, his paws on the controls, and the caption is "I have no idea what I'm doing." That one has always spoken to me.

My name is Brant, and I am that dog.

I'm a guy who's never had a Big Plan. I thought about titling this book *The Accidental Tourist*, but it sounded familiar so I looked it up, and that's the title of a Pulitzer Prize-winning novel. I'm glad I looked it up.

I do feel like I've been led on a tour over the years, and it's been a beautiful and profound one, even if I don't remember actually signing up for it. It's taken me through many countries now, from Afghanistan to Zambia. And it's allowed me to meet thousands of remarkable people, even if most of my meetings were not particularly smooth (see chapter 7, "About the Time My Face Hit a Parked Truck").

It's all been very unlikely, as is the fact that I'm writing a book to help you experience life to the fullest. Looking back, I'm not the person you would have picked to ever do that. You know how some people are just naturally the life of the party? That wasn't me. But as you'll see, I'm totally getting there.

Much of my life has been . . . awkward. I'm not adept socially. I'm on the autism spectrum. I'm from a broken family in rural Illinois. Working in radio and being a writer have been good fits for me because I have things to say but don't enjoy being seen.

This is because I've gone through life with a neurological condition called nystagmus, which causes some major social confusion. It causes my eyes and head to shake, like I'm always saying no to everybody. And, as it turns out, humans aren't magnetically drawn to someone they meet who is immediately indicating disapproval.[1]

When I was a kid, one of my hobbies was to go to my room, pull out my pens and crayons, and draw. I would draw very realistic maps of the US and would circle names of American cities. Then, based on my knowledge of Russian ballistic missile capabilities, I'd try to figure out the odds of my family surviving a nuclear war.

Other kids? Playing Atari or something. Me? I'm a little kid with thick glasses hovering alone over his homemade nuclear-fallout maps, wondering when we go to DEFCON 1.

The real question in my little brain was whether nuclear war would happen before another looming disaster: Judgment Day. I was also ever worried that the sky would split open, Jesus would show up, and I would face judgment on the spot. I'd surely be tried and found guilty. I'd accidentally said "What the hell?" during a game in our front yard with my older brother, Darin. I was scared and immediately conscience-stricken and begged him to never tell anyone. So far, to my knowledge, he's been solid on this. Thank

---

1. I've learned that in Romania they shake their heads back and forth to say yes. I now hope to move there and become a powerful motivational speaker.

you, Darin. But I knew *God* heard, and I was in big trouble when Jesus came back.

We were kids in the dysfunctional home of a pastor. My mom did the best she could, but it was a very frightening and dark place. I won't write much about this here, but please know that if we were to sit down for coffee and you heard a bit of my story (I'd rather ask you about yours, honestly), you'd likely ask what many others have: "How the heck are you still a believer in Jesus?"

By nature, I'm a bitter pessimist. A glass-half-empty guy. A fatalist. A very anxious person.

I'm telling you this because that's not me anymore.

Now, I'm still an "actually" guy. I was born that way and I'm keeping it going. I'm told I should fight this impulse, but I don't fully understand why. Don't people want correct information?

> THEM: Wow, I love this "Jingle Bells" song! It's our
>   favorite Christmas song!
> ME: *Actually*, it was written for Thanksgiving. It's not a
>   Christmas song, per se.
> THEM: . . .
> ME: You are welcome for this information.
> THEM: Please leave us.
> ME: Okay.

I've always felt like a misfit. I even wrote a book about that called *Blessed Are the Misfits*, which—speaking of Pulitzer Prizes!—hasn't won one.

So, with this impressive list of qualifications in mind, please consider me your own virtual tour guide for the rest of this book. It will be an epic and bold, courageous journey of adventure and discovery and also footnotes of dubious value.[2]

---

2. Like this one.

I simply want to tell you about some people I've met and some beautiful things I'm so thankful I've been able to witness, especially given how I grew up. Maybe you're like this too. Maybe you need to see something fresh.

I want to show you why, even as someone prone to great skepticism, I am gaining faith when so many other people in our culture seem to be losing it. These are things I've been able to see, and maybe you need to see them too.

> I want to show you why, even as someone prone to great skepticism, I am gaining faith when so many other people in our culture seem to be losing it.

They point toward a single prize, a single gift. I think you'll love it.

After all, I'm convinced you're yearning for it. We all are. Every single human who's ever walked this planet is looking for it, deep down.

It's available to us right now.

It's called *joy*.

ONE

"The Second Naivete": The Chapter That Combines a French Philosopher and *The Dukes of Hazzard*

*Joy isn't based on ignorance,
it's about knowing more.*

Once, there was a big boat. There were precisely 276 people on board, and precisely 275 of them were freaking out. They knew the boat was going down. The storm was way too much.

They gave up hope entirely. "We're totally going to drown!" they said. But then there was one guy who was totally calm. It wasn't the captain, or some other veteran sailor who'd seen it all. No, all the salty professionals were freaking out too.

So, you wonder: *Was this calm guy an idiot? Couldn't he see the obvious?* To not be anxious in the middle of all that, you'd have to lack basic knowledge about how the world works, right?

Turns out the guy—Paul, in the Bible—wasn't an idiot. He didn't lack knowledge. No, he was calm because he knew *more* than everyone else on board. He told them the ship would go down but everyone would survive and be just fine. And so it did, and so they were. (It's in Acts 27–28.)

I tell you this story because in our culture now it's kind of like we're all in a big boat, and everyone's freaking out. Anxiety and anger are so widespread that if you're not anxious and angry, people will suspect it's because you're willfully ignorant of all the Big Issues. You just don't know, or you don't care, because if you did, you'd be just as scared and ticked off as they are.

I've noticed people will get angry if I'm not angry enough about the things they happen to be angry about. They think I don't care. Or they think I'm naive at best. "Don't you know about this crisis, and that injustice, and this other tragedy?"

But then there it is, this joy thing, and I love how Dallas Willard defined it: Joy is "not a passing sensation of pleasure, but a pervasive sense of well-being."[1] No matter what happens, that sense of well-being is there.

It might seem impossible or even crazy to live this way in a world of anger and anxiety. But I want you to know that it's possible. And not only that, I want you to know that joy is quite reasonable, in light of reality properly understood. Jesus kept showing His followers that too.

> Joy is "a pervasive sense of well-being."

Yes, horrible things happen. Yes, there is great evil in the world. But joy—this sense of well-being—doesn't come from knowing less.

Joy comes from knowing *more*.

✦

You know what? Maybe joyful people *are* naive. But it's not the kind of naivete that means just plain uninformed. It's a different naive.

French philosopher Paul Ricoeur wrote about a "second naivete," one that exists on the far side of complexity. I think he's onto something.

When you're young and naive, like a little kid, you can believe in a simple, beautiful thing. You might then spend much of your life questioning it, doubting it, criticizing it, complexifying it, maybe even smirking at people who still believe that simple, beautiful thing. And then you just might, down the line, realize that the simple, beautiful thing *was* and *is* true. And then you just might, even further down the line, be able to marvel again and wonder.

"Some day," C. S. Lewis wrote, "you will be old enough to start reading fairy tales again."[2]

There was a world-renowned theologian named Karl Barth who was famously asked a question toward the end of his epic career. A student wanted to know if he could sum up his entire life's theological work in just a sentence.

He said yes, he could. "In the words of a song I learned at my mother's knee: 'Jesus loves me, this I know, for the Bible tells me so.'"[3]

I've learned that simple things aren't stupid things. It's complexity that often masks foolishness with the veneer of intelligence.

I once took a religious studies class on Judaism in Nazi Germany. Each week, we had to write a paper on the subject. I thought, *I can write. This will be no problem.*

But it was a problem. The professor looked at my papers and ripped my writing to pieces. It was brutal. He had a side gig writing dictionary definitions, it turns out, and he was quite gifted at finding every single extra word and crossing it out with a red pen. He wanted precision and concision. He was relentless, he was unsparing, and you know what else he was? He was right.

I was extra wordy because I wanted to sound impressive.

I've learned simplicity is beautiful, but often it demands far more of us than does complexity. It reminds me of a long letter from Blaise Pascal, the famous mathematician and philosopher, in which he wrote, "I have made this [letter] longer than usual, only because I have not had time to make it shorter."[4]

So no, simple things aren't stupid things. Sometimes things are simple because we have more understanding, not less.

Like when I was a kid and I earnestly thought quicksand was going to be an existential threat throughout my entire life. I knew I'd always need to be looking out for it, or surely it would eventually get me.

Why did I believe this? For fun, do a quick search of "quicksand" and "TV" and you get episodes of *The Dukes of Hazzard*, *Batman*, *I Love Lucy*, *The Six Million Dollar Man*, *Tarzan*, *Fantasy Island*, *Gilligan's Island*, *The Fall Guy*, *The Bionic Woman*, *One Life to Live*, *JAG*, *The Incredible Hulk* . . . It goes on and on. Everyone, everywhere, all the time, was constantly sinking in quicksand.

> I've learned simplicity is beautiful, but often it demands far more of us than does complexity.

It's a complicating thing in life, this worrying about the threat of suddenly, yet slowly, sinking into the ground. But I now know more, like the fact that statistically quicksand kills . . . pretty much no one, ever.[5] I do not need to be scared of quicksand.

Nerdy eight-year-old me would have protested at first—What? Can this be true?—but ultimately I would have been so relieved. No more nightmares about that. I could go back to just drawing nuclear-fallout maps.

+

I believe we lack joy not because we now know too much but because we know too little.

Or we've forgotten what we knew.

Think about it: Jesus basically said in John 16:33, "Yes, I know you will have problems. I know. But here's some additional information that might interest you—something I know but you don't . . ."

And then He told us to be of good cheer.

God is quite aware of all the suffering and injustice, thank you; but if we believe what Jesus believes, we'll have a sense of well-being no matter what.

Yes, pain is real. Suffering is real. But in Jesus' worldview, despair is not the deepest reality. We know it is a fleeting thing. It's joy that underpins everything. It's the deepest note that rings through our lives, even in tragedy.

We'll hurt, we'll cry, we'll go through tremendous loss. We might be deeply unhappy. And yet . . . His peace persists.

So yes, there is a "second naivete," a second *simplicity*. It's an innocence and a beautiful, peaceful life we can live in light of what we can know.

Like, say, how this all ends.

+

I grew up in little towns in Illinois and Indiana. They were very flat, windy, and cold. And in late winter, we'd see little crocus flowers poking up through the snow. It was about this time of year, too, we'd hear about baseball players gathering in the sun in Florida, and we'd go find our mitts in the garage and get ready. We knew that first sixty-degree day would come soon.

I love what Tim Mackie from BibleProject said about that: he said it's a good example of what simple faith really is.[6] Yes, it's something that hasn't happened yet—something we can't fully see yet—but we base our actions on it.

We know what's coming. The tiny flowers are poking through.

We have faith, not because we don't have reasons but because we do.

TWO

Not in This for the T-Shirt

Why religious hypocrisy hasn't chased me from Jesus.

She was looking at her own face. She was transfixed.

I had taken out my iPhone, fumbled with it for a second, and reversed the camera, so it worked like a mirror. And I handed it to her.

She was seventeen years old, and she'd lived her entire life as a pariah. She was considered a freak and a curse. She'd never gone to a day of school. She only rarely saw the light of day outside the walls of her small home. Her parents were frightened they'd be cast out of the community if others knew they'd been cursed with such a being.

We were sitting in a hospital ward in Kabul, Afghanistan, and she had just had a surgery to repair her cleft palate. Her lips were swollen, and there were stitches, but her face was finally whole.

She looked dramatically different from the young woman I'd seen before her surgery.

When she took my phone, she held it silently in front of her. And she couldn't stop looking. She just gazed . . . and gazed . . . in amazement.

She's no freak, of course. She never was. Every girl wants to be beautiful, and she was seeing something deeply beautiful.

So was I.

I was seeing an advance trailer of heaven.

✦

It's fair to ask, "Okay, so how did you wind up in a hospital in Afghanistan?" And honestly, I just kind of bumbled into it. That's my MO: I bumble into stuff. It started with me being forced to emcee a concert, something that horrifies me, to be honest. I'm the last person you want as a hype man, but since I'm a radio host, I sometimes have no choice.

True story: I had to emcee an outdoor, daytime TobyMac show at a Miami amphitheater. I tried to get the audience excited when I introduced Toby . . . but he didn't come out onstage.

I was confused and alarmed. The concert promoters, using walkie-talkies to talk to other people backstage, told me to go back out. "He's ready now!" they said. So I did. I went back onstage and tried to make a joke out of it and get the crowd hyped again (they were a little more reserved now), and then I introduced him again. "Please welcome, *TobyMac*!"

He and his band did not come out. Again.

I was now mortified. This is an introvert's worst nightmare. I wanted to leave, but they told me there was a mix-up, not Toby's fault. But for real—he's ready this time. Just one more time, go back out there and announce him.

I slinked back out, tried to make a joke of it again, no one laughed. People were tired of me. But I introduced him again.

And I'm here to tell you that once again he did *not* come out.

I walked to the side of the stage and silently grabbed my phone and keys, and the crowd watched as I walked down the stairs from the band shell and then into the parking lot behind the stage, where I got into my car and then drove home.

I presume he came out at some point, but I don't know. Maybe everybody's still there.

+

Anyway, at another concert—they just keep doing this to me—I was asked to make an onstage announcement about CURE. I had no idea what CURE was. I asked a woman representing CURE what it was, and she told me the basic story.

There are millions of kids around the world who have disabilities that could be fixed with surgery . . . but they don't get fixed. So a married couple who are Jesus followers, one a nurse and the other an orthopedic surgeon, thought, *Well . . . why don't we fix them? Jesus told us to proclaim the kingdom and heal the sick. Shouldn't that be what we're known for?* CURE grew into a network of permanent surgical hospitals serving the poorest of the poor, children who would never get access to surgeries otherwise.

I liked that. I'm like a lot of people (maybe you?) who honestly want to see Jesus in action. Not just talked about. Not marketed or sold. I've had enough of that. I'm weary of the hype. I want to see Jesus stuff *actually happen.*

CURE told me they might be building a hospital in Palestine, and since one of the things I do is host a radio show, I thought it might be a cool thing to visit around Christmas. I could go to the hospital and help them raise funds for surgeries or something.

Then, months later, the wrinkle: "We're afraid that hospital isn't happening right now. So . . . how about you go to our hospital in Afghanistan?"

My first reaction: "How about *no* . . . ?"

My wife, Carolyn, and I talked about it at length. She was understandably concerned but also excited about what CURE was doing and how we might be able to be part of it somehow.

I found myself on a plane to Kabul, and then in an operating room watching this young woman's face be made whole. When I handed her my iPhone, I silently thanked God, knowing that, through His people, He had just rewritten her life story.

✦

Maybe this is true for you too: lately I've been reading a lot of manifestos by people, usually religious celebrities, who are publicly announcing they're leaving the faith or on their way out the door. They've deconstructed and found they have nothing left.

I do understand where they are coming from. I've seen toxic religion so up close and personal it hurts. As I mentioned, I get this a lot from people who know how I grew up, in a pastor's home filled with terrifying religious hypocrisy: "How in the world did you wind up a Jesus follower?"

It's a fine question.

I've seen such deep ugliness, and not just as a kid. I've seen how professional Christians have transformed so much of "church" into an industry. I've seen people drag Jesus into their political power plays, on the Left and Right. Working in Christian music radio, I've had to protest plans to mislead listeners for fundraising purposes, and I've even quit jobs over it.

I counted the other day—full-time church pastors I've personally known who have cheated on their wives and been found out: fourteen so far, including my dad.

In several incidents, I've been treated dismissively by religious leaders and preachers . . . until they find out I have a platform, which is when I'm suddenly richly deserving of their time and attention.

Ugh.

I've had to do more than a little deconstruction myself, reconsidering what Jesus had in mind for His church and determining what being His disciple means and what it doesn't. I've asked questions about my own motives. Sometimes I've felt like I'm barely hanging on.

But I'm not writing a manifesto or a declaration. (If I did, I would use a quill because quills are cool.) But my point is, I'm not going to write one, because here's something I've noticed about these "I'm leaving Christianity" statements, something very, very odd: *they don't mention Jesus.*

Or His kingdom.

You see, this King, and this kingdom, are the reasons I can't leave. So I'm always left wondering, *Okay, I get the critique. Makes sense. But . . . what about Jesus? Isn't that what you were here for? And you don't even mention Him?*

Honestly, if Jesus were just a side issue, I could understand why you'd leave Christianity. I'm not in this for the Christian pop culture or even the T-shirts, including the "Lord's Gym" one where Jesus is doing push-ups with the cross on His back and it says, "Bench Press This!" Not even that one. I'm not in it for that. That's not enough.

I'm not in it for the Christian movies, either, including the one with the guy from *Growing Pains* who works as a fireman, although I bet it was probably a good movie. Maybe. I don't know. My point is, I'm not in this for that.

There's rarely a day on social media when I don't read about some Christian leader doing something scandalous, stupid, or just plain embarrassing. Then I'll see equally embarrassing comments and posts in response from people I know. I feel like I can spend a good portion of the day face-palming. I, like many before me, ask myself whether I seriously want to be associated with this lunacy. What in the world?!

The cultural tide is strong, it's pulling the other way, and if my experience of the Christian thing was based on weekly worship concerts with fog machines or church-camp memories or the mega-scandal of the day or politely served chicken sandwiches—however zesty—well, I'm out of here too.

But I'm convinced of this: Once we've seen the reality of the kingdom of God, it's very hard to walk away. It's just too good.

Even people like me, people who are cynical by nature or struggle to be spiritual in some emotional way—once we get it, nothing else will do.

> Once we've seen the reality of the kingdom of God, it's very hard to walk away. It's just too good.

There's a lot of religious baggage and immature thinking that can and should be "left behind." And when people tell me, "Don't criticize the church; Jesus would never criticize the church," I get confused because there's Jesus in Revelation 2 taking churches to the woodshed.

I've opted out of a lot of pop religion. What I won't do is walk away from this kingdom. No way.

Jesus talked about a pearl merchant, a man who really knew his business, who recognized what was truly valuable. And then he found it! A pearl worth everything he had. So he made his move. He had to have it. He sold everything to get it.

In another parable, Jesus said the kingdom is like a treasure hidden in a field. A guy found the treasure, then hid it again. Why?

So he could go sell everything and buy that field. He had to get the treasure.

The pearl merchant, the treasure-field guy—they were not fools. Quite the opposite.

The kingdom is just too appealing, too poetic, too stunning. The alternatives grow dingy in its light. If you know what's life-and-death valuable, well, you just *have* to have it.

It's always kind of baffled me when Jesus talked about the kingdom in Matthew and said "violent people" raid it. My understanding now is that He was referring to an eagerness to have it; some people will seize it. I've also heard it compared to the eagerness cows have to be let into a fresh, new green pasture after a long winter.[1]

So yes, I can talk about the abuses and weirdness of religion and things done in the name of Jesus. But I'm not leaving Jesus or my brothers and sisters who seek Him.

There may be fewer of us in the days ahead, at least in the US, where I live. But I feel now I've become like Jesus' friends, the ones who stayed after everyone else walked away from Him. Jesus turned to them and asked, "You do not want to leave too, do you?" (John 6:67).

Nope.

Where else do I go? No one else has the words of life.

And no one else offers this joy, this peace, this sense of well-being regardless of circumstances. No one. The alternatives, I'm convinced, don't work.

I can't leave, because now I've seen too much, including a lot of things I'm going to tell you about in this book. I'm not going anywhere. Yes, there are religious hypocrites in the world. But I'm

---

1. Look it up on YouTube: when the gates swing open, the cows dance with glee, and now I realize I totally should have had a photo of that on the cover of this book, and maybe changed the title: *Life Is Hard. God Is Good. Check Out These Awesome Cows.*

Yes, there are religious hypocrites in the world. But I'm not going to give them the power to stop me from the best relationship of my life.

not going to give them the power to stop me from the best relationship of my life.

This gospel, this good news that the kingdom is now available to all of us? It's too good to trade in for a sweet rush of very temporary freedom. Jesus makes too much sense. I *have* to trust someone—we all do—so really: Who better than Jesus?

I've seen what happens when people actually do what Jesus told us to do, like, say, making a seventeen-year-old girl's dream come true.

The kingdom is beyond beautiful. Shocking, even. When you see it, you might just gaze . . . and gaze . . . in amazement.

THREE

Nobody Moves into Assumption, Illinois

God's personality might be better than you think.

Assumption isn't a horrible place. It's just that it's barely there. Those who do know of its existence either live there or drive around it on Route 51 on their way to Decatur and make jokes about the name of the town.

Assumption is a tiny, working-class village built on the pure, unbroken flatness of central Illinois.[1] Assumption has no stoplights. It doesn't even have a four-way stop. No, for four-way-stop action, you need to go seven miles north to hoity-toity Moweaqua.

I played in the Assumption Little League, which was a few dozen kids who played one another over and over. I was baseball

---

1. Our go-to dad joke: one day, the wind stopped, and all our cows fell over.

crazy, even though I was terrible at it. One reason I think I was terrible at baseball is because I couldn't actually, you know, see the baseball. I never quite knew where it was until it hit my body.

But I played anyway, even with a shaking head and profound nearsightedness. I loved baseball statistics so much I just had to be part of the game. My stats? I batted .000 for my eight-year baseball career.[2]

But that's a whole other story. Please know it's not very action-packed.

I was also extremely lonely.

My parents had just gotten a divorce. Since my dad was the pastor of Assumption Christian Church, everyone knew what had happened. I felt humiliated. What's more, we had to move out of our house. It was the church parsonage. My dad left town, and my mom found a very old, very tiny home—maybe five hundred square feet?—for her; my older brother, Darin; and me.

Mom slept in the living room on the couch. My brother and I had bunk beds.

One night I distinctly remember, in the dark of the bottom bunk, crying from loneliness. I didn't cry often. I didn't want my brother to hear me. But I cried and asked God, "Please, please send me a friend."

That's it. I think it was as pure a prayer as I've ever mustered. And if it sounds like a sad story, it's not.

Because *the very next day* (not exaggerating) at Little League practice, something that never happens . . . happened. A new kid showed up: Robbie. He and his mom and brother had just moved into Assumption.

Forty years later, Rob and I still text each other and laugh about anything and everything.

---

2. For fellow advanced-stat enthusiasts, my bWAR was 0.0, my "slash line" was .000/.000 /.000, and I had an OPS+ of—punches numbers furiously on calculator—ah yes, 0.

Robbie was obsessed with baseball statistics. He didn't have great social skills. (He now admits that, yes, maybe he's on the spectrum too.) He was crazy smart. And his parents had also recently gotten divorced.

When we weren't together doing tabletop baseball simulations and developing our own analytics, we would talk on the phone, often for more than an hour, strictly about baseball stats. Nothing else.

Both of our moms would overhear the conversations and wonder, *Why is my son so odd? And where in the world did this other odd boy come from?*

Rob and I were best friends all through middle school and high school, and we'll never not be friends. Too many memories, too many laughs, too much in common. We still talk baseball. He's still my go-to guy. He's also a history nerd and follows the way of Jesus.

He now lives in fancy Moweaqua, the town with the four-way stop, where he became a teacher, administrator, and state-championship-level basketball coach. Even though we don't live near each other, he's the kind of friend you have internal discussions with. I can still imagine his reactions to things and what he'd say. Maybe you can relate to that. It's a remarkable thing.

I so remember that night, that one summer night in a tiny room in a tiny home in a tiny village. My brother and I had a box fan running in the window, but I could still hear the train rumbling through the middle of town. I remember the silent crying, and the asking, and the yearning. It's vivid. It was pure heartbreak.

I now believe God is really this good: I think He heard the outcry of a lonely, misfit boy and said, *Okay. I hear you. I've got this. I'm sending in Robbie.*

Someone moving *into* Assumption? A baseball-stats savant? And the very next day? What are the odds of that?

I tell you this story partly because I want to encourage you to pray, out loud, honestly. Simply. Clearly.

But mostly I'm writing this just because I'm thankful, and it's good to rehearse stories of God's faithfulness. Why do I sometimes suspect He doesn't care or doesn't listen? One honest prayer and I'm still benefiting forty years later.

I figure if God listened to a desperate kid in Assumption, Illinois, maybe He'll listen to other desperate people anytime, anywhere. Including you.

✦

A friend of mine once said something I've been thinking about ever since: "Everyone, whether they admit it or not, believes in God. It's just that many don't *trust* Him." Deep down, they don't think He's truly good or that He could really be *for* them.

I think my friend could be right. I suppose it all comes down to what we think about when we think about God. If you read the stories about Jesus in the Bible, you'll see Him constantly trying to get people to *re*-think (literally what "repent" means) what they think they know about God and how He works.

Rethinking is hard. Shoot, *thinking* is hard. But getting people to reconsider stuff? Almost impossible. Maybe that's why Jesus kept saying to crowds, "If just one of you would repent, all of heaven would throw a massive party" (Luke 15:7).

We don't usually like being told we need to rethink, but there's Jesus, telling us to do it. He's telling us we need to update our imaginations about God. (Notice all the times He said stuff like "You've heard it said . . . ," and then "but I tell you . . .")

Weirdly, people resented it even though Jesus was saying, in so many different ways, "Look, folks: God is better than you think. You can trust Him. Because of Him, you're safe in this world. You can go all in with Him. Even in the worst-case scenario: He's still got you."

Many won't believe it. Rethinking is so hard, we'll often choose anxiety and anger instead.

I saw an article on the tech site Gizmodo called "7 Moments in the Bible When Jesus Acted Very Un-Jesus-Like."[1] From the writer's perspective, it was out of character for Jesus to do the stuff Jesus did. That's like all of us, I guess: we have an idea what God is like, and we're not going to let anyone or anything, including God Himself, get in the way of it.

Lord, we ask You to politely stay in the idiom we have made for You. Amen.

But think about it: What if He's *better?* What if He has a particular personality, and it's a great one? Honestly: Would I want to get to know Him more, or just stick with my presumptions? What if having the right ideas about who God really is would give us a sense of well-being that could go with us anywhere and through absolutely anything?

I want to keep learning. I know I need to. I hope you see in this book how good God really is, and that you're in a much better place when you realize you can fully trust Him. To learn, we must be humble about what we know, and what we don't.

I love this prayer from Thomas Merton. Maybe you will too:

My Lord God, I have no idea where I am going. I do not see the road ahead of me. I cannot know for certain where it will end. Nor do I really know myself, and the fact that I think I am following your will does not mean that I am actually doing so. But I believe that the desire to please you does in fact please you. And I hope I have that desire in all that I am doing. I hope that I will never do anything apart from that desire. And I know that if I do this you will lead me by the right road, though I may know nothing about it. Therefore I will trust you always though I may seem to be lost and in the shadow of death. I will not fear, for you are ever with me, and you will never leave me to face my perils alone.[2]

He promises He will hear us when we humbly cry out to Him. I can vouch for that.[3]

---

3. Weird and awesome: I got a random funny message from Rob while I was typing these last two sentences.

FOUR

For He Hath Brought
Forth a Cushion

We don't need to be anxious, even if the ship goes down.

I still love playing games, even if I'm terrible at them. I suspect most adults want to play more but want to seem "professional" or "dignified" or something, but I am clearly unburdened by this desire for professionalism and dignity.

When it comes to playing, I don't mess around. I'm all in, every time. Whether it's chess or flag football or tag or Hungry Hungry Hippos, I leave it all on the field.

So when I was a counselor at a summer day camp for little elementary-aged kids, my enthusiasm was probably alarming even to some of the kids. Kickball? I'm kicking towering homer after homer, trotting around the bases, and doing a Tim Tebow kneel after I cross home plate. That's how I play the game. I usually act as the play-by-play announcer, too ("and Hansen goes deep *again!*"), and the kids love that. I think.

Anyway, once we were playing follow-the-leader with the kids on a playground, and it was my turn to lead. I sprinted around the swing set, and everyone ran after me in an enthusiastic line. I jumped over a low balance beam, and everyone did the same thing. I darted up a ladder to the top of a tallish slide. I then decided to run, not slide, down the slide, which would have been totally cool if not for the tripping, which led to my body flying down and off the slide, out of control, and then bouncing across the gravel playground, like a skipping stone, before finally coming to rest, nestled peacefully at the foot of a bench under a tree.

I lay for a second and thought about all the places where I might be scraped. I thought about how I had just effectively exfoliated my entire body.

I looked up from the ground and saw the disturbed and now silent children. The little boy who was in line directly behind me was standing atop the slide, looking down in total shock.

"We . . . we . . . have to do . . . *that?*"

Honestly, I suspected following Jesus would mean something like this. Following sounds okay, maybe, but . . . *where are we going, really?* I mean, at some point there's going to be something He wants me to do that's . . . terrifying. Like being tortured on the medieval rack for my beliefs, or sent to a gulag, or maybe made to serve as a greeter at church.

This gets back to the trust thing, I suppose. Yes, maybe I believe there's a god, but I don't trust that god as much as I trust me. I think that's where most people actually are. Maybe they'd really resonate with this book if I tweaked the title to *Life Is Hard.*

God Is Probably Kinda Sketchy. Let's Be Anxious but Try Not to Think About It.

But if I can really trust Him, everything changes. We all can imagine worst-case scenarios. We're good at it, getting stressed and anxious about things that haven't happened and might never happen.

But what if you could know that even if the worst-case scenarios happen, you'd somehow be okay? That sounds crazy, but I'm convinced this is exactly what Jesus is telling us. There is seriously nothing in this world that can ultimately endanger you.

Like Dallas Willard said, for people who trust God, "our universe is *a perfectly safe place for us to be.*"[1]

Willard was just agreeing with Jesus. Jesus told us we don't need to spend a minute worrying about the future. Yes, He's fully aware of how the world works. He's aware of the realities of deprivation and injustice and disease and death. He's not ignorant, He's the smartest man of all time.

> **What if you could know that even if the worst-case scenarios happen, you'd somehow be okay?**

JESUS: Do you believe that I know more than you?

US: Yes, infinitely more.

JESUS: Good. Now you'll believe Me when I tell you that you don't have to worry about anything.

US: But what about X and Y?

JESUS: Oh, I know about X and Y. But I also know Z! It's good news!

US: But X and Y!

JESUS: Right, but Z!

US: But X and Y tho!

JESUS: (*Sighs.*)

US: (*Turns on TV.*)
TV NEWS HOSTS: X and Y, folks. X and Y and also Y
and X . . .

✦

Maybe you've heard the "Jesus calms the storm" story before. But really think about it: Jesus got in a boat with His disciples, and they took off across a big lake. They got hit by a storm, everybody panicked—except one guy, again. They found Jesus "sleeping on a cushion," and they woke Him up, and He asked everybody, "Why are you so afraid?" and then He calmed the storm (Mark 4).

Two things stand out to me:

1. *This whole trip was Jesus' idea!* He was taking them on a follow-the-leader trip to show they don't ever need to worry about anything.
2. *Jesus slept on a cushion.* The writer, Mark, is known for being the least detailed writer of the entire Bible. He's all big picture and big action. And he mentioned a . . . cushion?

I just checked, and it's the only time "cushion" is mentioned in the sixty-six books of the Bible. What's my takeaway here? I don't know. Not everything has a takeaway, maybe. Or maybe Jesus usually packed His own cushion. My wife brings her pillow everywhere.

Jesus was showing the disciples something that, if we trust Him, will allow us to live a life in a wonderfully free way: Even if the ship goes down, we'll be safe. If we are with Him, we're safe. Death itself is not the last word.

The last word is *joy.*

Of course, there will be times when we should mourn. Yes, grief

will visit us. Yes, pain is part of our existence. Yes to all of that. But this will pass.

Jesus is giving us eternal life, and
while most of us might think He's talking about what starts after we're dead,
that's not what He's talking about at
all. He's talking about a *quality* of life
available to us right now.

Jesus was showing
the disciples
something that, if we
trust Him, will allow
**us to live a life in a
wonderfully free way.**

But what if it's all going down? For real. Like everything is
falling apart. What if the country falls to pieces? What if the evil
people are winning? What if I lose everything? Shouldn't I be anxious *then*?

Nope. No need.

Can anyone really live like that? Yes. I give you Jeremiah, writing after his nation—his way of life, everything—was gone. Check
out how he felt. There's some gut-level honesty here:

> I have been deprived of peace;
> I have forgotten what prosperity is.
> So I say, "My splendor is gone
> and all that I had hoped from the LORD."
> I remember my affliction and my wandering,
> the bitterness and the gall.
> I well remember them,
> and my soul is downcast within me.

Yeah. I think I'd feel that way. But watch what he did next: he
deliberately *remembered*.

> Yet this I call to mind
> and therefore I have hope:
> Because of the LORD's great love we are not consumed,

for his compassions never fail.

They are new every morning;

great is your faithfulness.

I say to myself, "The LORD is my portion;

therefore I will wait for him." (Lamentations 3:17–24)

Does it sound like he's talking to himself? It should, because he's talking to himself. He's reminding himself that there's more to the story. There's more than what meets the eye.

Ultimately, he's telling himself, "Wait: I know this God. I know He's good. I know I can trust Him. No matter what."

Jeremiah was secure. Not because he was blissfully unaware but because he was *very* aware. He was the opposite of ignorant. He knew more.

As an author who is under contract to make as many allusions to C. S. Lewis as possible, I can't help but bring up Narnia again, specifically Lucy from *The Voyage of the Dawn Treader*, who cries out to Aslan in mortal fear. She feels frightened and alone. She's on a ship bound for utter darkness. Aslan—the lion who represents Jesus in the books—answers her.

There's a sudden stream of light, and Lucy looks to the sky to see an albatross over the ship, flying and singing a comforting song. "No one except Lucy knew that as it circled the mast it had whispered to her, 'Courage, dear heart,' and the voice, she felt sure, was Aslan's, and with the voice a delicious smell breathed in her face."[2]

It's nice to know the story ends with the ship being led to safety. But knowing this is even better: *In real life, even if the ship goes down, I don't need to be scared.* My feelings may say otherwise, but my feelings have been known to lie.

Why? This God is good. I have to remind myself: I can trust Him. Really.

Courage, dear heart.

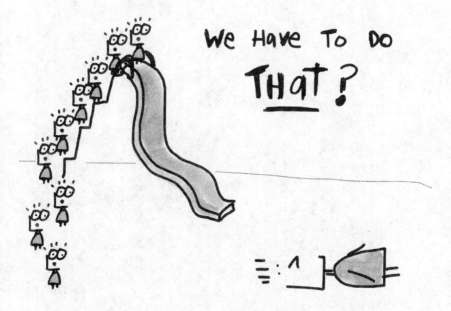

FIVE

A Genius Idea:
Outsource Your Worry

Jesus is not unrealistic in telling us not to be anxious.

Speaking of trusting God: there remain many things I just don't get.

I have questions.

Perhaps you're with me on this: What's with the bugs? I can easily imagine a universe without mosquitoes, for example. And a related question from the bourgeoning discipline of theo-entomo-eschatological studies: *Will bugs be in heaven?*

People are pretty sure dogs will be in heaven. I agree with them. Since it will be a restored creation, a new heaven and new earth, it will be highly recognizable and highly enjoyable. Trees, lakes, streams, dogs. All of it.

But bugs?

My guess? Yes. There probably will be bugs, but not without some sort of accounting from them. Before there's reconciliation, mosquitoes are going to need to explain why they kept attacking my ankles for decades. I'm not going to act like that didn't just happen.

For now, I see dimly, but I must trust that there's some deeply good reason for the existence of mosquitoes. I must trust the Creator, while continuing to slap and spray His creation.

Trust and kill. For there's no other way.

✦

I was reading a book about being efficient and getting things all the way done. I got only about halfway, but I do remember something: the author offered tips on getting help by *outsourcing*.

He'd hire people in other countries, and they'd take care of his stuff, everything from dealing with clients to setting up dental appointments.

He was under a lot of pressure, and as a kind of joke he asked his assistant in India to worry for him. He gave her a list of a few things he was worried about, and she said, "Okay, I'll worry about those things for you today."

What's even weirder: the guy said it worked! Just knowing someone was out there, somewhere, worrying in his stead? It somehow put him more at ease. He would set those things aside and concentrate on things he could control that day.

This is kind of goofy, but that's how our minds work. We want some sense of control over the future, and at some level, worrying gives it to us. Maybe paying someone in India to worry for you can give you that same sense.

But there's an even better way. "Outsourcing our worries" may be an absolutely brilliant way to think about our trusting relationship with God. I mean, it's scriptural.

The verse literally says, "Give all your worries and cares to God, for he cares about you" (1 Peter 5:7 NLT). Throw them to Him. Let Him deal with them, instead of you.

We can hire someone in India to do it for you, and that apparently has a bit of benefit. But imagine handing it over to someone really powerful, like, say, the Creator of the universe. He can do things!

This sounds like a very good deal. I need to do this more. I'm learning just how helpful it is in having peace. As I learn He's truly good, and believe the things about Him that Jesus believes, I trust Him more to handle things.

✦

Speaking of control: We love it. We want it so bad. We can't imagine being without it. Even when we can't have it, we want to pretend we have it.

I have seen empirical evidence of this on vivid display. It happens when humans gather to upend club-shaped wooden objects arranged in a triangle on the floor. You grab a heavy ball and roll it down a long, varnished runway in hopes of knocking them over. It's called bowling, and it starts with renting shoes other people have just worn and I'd never really thought about that until I put on a pair and *they were still warm* and I don't want to think about this anymore really.

> We love control.
> We want it so bad.
> We can't imagine being without it. Even when we can't have it, we want to pretend we have it.

The fascinating thing, beyond that we're willing to do the gross shoe-rental thing, is what happens once humans release the ball. We lean and gyrate and gesticulate and turn, even though it has no effect whatsoever on what's happening. I mean, the ball is gone. We should really let it go.

In life, it's really better if we just do what we can . . . and then outsource the worry. We did our thing; now, Lord, please do Yours.

Psychologists say we think worrying will help us be more prepared for something catastrophic or make us better at solving a problem we're facing. But neither is true, they say. We're just leaning over and hoping that helps steer the bowling ball toward the pins.

Jesus, who knows a thing or two about how we function best, told us that worrying is a waste:

> "Therefore I tell you, do not worry about your life, what you will eat or drink; or about your body, what you will wear. Is not life more than food, and the body more than clothes? Look at the birds of the air; they do not sow or reap or store away in barns, and yet your heavenly Father feeds them. Are you not much more valuable than they? Can any one of you by worrying add a single hour to your life?
>
> "And why do you worry about clothes? See how the flowers of the field grow. They do not labor or spin. Yet I tell you that not even Solomon in all his splendor was dressed like one of these. If that is how God clothes the grass of the field, which is here today and tomorrow is thrown into the fire, will he not much more clothe you—you of little faith? So do not worry, saying, 'What shall we eat?' or 'What shall we drink?' or 'What shall we wear?' For the pagans run after all these things, and your heavenly Father knows that you need them. But seek first his kingdom and his righteousness, and all these things will be given to you as well. Therefore do not worry about tomorrow, for tomorrow will worry about itself. Each day has enough trouble of its own." (Matthew 6:25–34)

Jesus was not a crazy man. He was not being idealistic. He was telling us how to live. He knows what He's talking about. It's entirely realistic. In fact, it's the ultimate in realistic because, in Jesus' view, the kingdom of God is the realest thing in the universe. It's the one thing that can't be shaken.

You can't lose it. He said seek it first and you're golden. You're safe.

"As long as we are worrying," James Bryan Smith wrote, "we can't seek first the kingdom of God. As long as we are seeking first the kingdom of God, we can't worry."[1]

But again, what about the evils of government? What about injustice? What about persecution? What about unfairness? What about poverty? What about racism? What about wars? What about infanticide? What about misogyny? What about illegal government occupation? What about all the immorality? What about all the oppression?

Was Jesus unaware of these things when He told us not to worry?

No, Jesus was not unaware of these things. Neither was His immediate audience. It was all part of their lives, all part of the first-century Roman world. If Jesus had been born into our current setting, I doubt He would change His tune and go with "Oh, wow. Yeah, okay, now *this* is seriously messed up. You have some legit worries here. Yikes, you guys."

If anything, I imagine people in the first century A.D. had more to worry about. For starters: Their life spans were shorter. The food supply was far more uncertain. They didn't have vaccines or antibiotics. And yet there Jesus was, telling people to trust God. Be like little animals. They're just concerned about today and what's directly in front of them. You'll have troubles, remember? But be of good cheer.

Lately, when I start feeling stressed about something that may happen tomorrow or next week or whenever, I picture sitting at a desk and having someone hand me a package that says "The Future" on it. And this mail is glowing. For some reason I have a Geiger counter on my desk and it's ticking. This thing is radioactive.

So I say, "Hey, this isn't for me. Not my department." So they take it away to the Radioactive Mail Department that easily and expertly handles that stuff. The future is not my deal. Not my department. I'm about today's stuff. Next!

Maybe it's a simplistic or goofy little image, of course, but it helps me. I have to remember: "Not my department. Not my department." Over and over. "Be like the birds," Jesus said. They don't kid themselves about how powerful they are or that they control the future.

$$+$$

How remarkable is it that Jesus is described as God's word made flesh in Scripture (John 1:14)? That means He's God's opinion. And God's opinion, for what it's worth to you, is that you have nothing to fear at all.

I've got my own opinions, but I'm going with His on this.

SIX

A Place Where God Walks the Earth

Finding joy in "blasts from the future."

Speaking of the future: It's something to be excited about. Giddy, even.[1]

This is surely why Jesus made healing such a big deal. He didn't have to. He could've just picked a miracle, any miracle. The King James Version could have included something like this:

> "Checketh this out," he spake. "For I hath fashioned 'dancing fountains' out of the Dead Sea, with lights and everything, and lo, they shalt be synchronized with music in a manner not unlike EPCOT foretold by the prophets."

---

1. I think that's the first time I've ever typed "giddy." It feels okay. Not great, but okay.

43

That's a dumb example, but seriously: Why *healing*? It didn't have to be so, right? There are a million more spectacular ideas to prove He had power, right? But He's not showing off His power. He's showing us what the future has in store.

It's like the realization I had when watching the girl in Afghanistan marvel at her new face following the surgery to correct her cleft palate: Jesus is giving us an advance trailer of heaven.

✦

A few weeks ago, the sun was setting in Lusaka, Zambia, and I stood with some friends near a playground. There were two little girls giggling and hopping along, their moms watching nearby.

We started talking to the moms and eventually playing with the little girls. They were new friends. Both were five years old, and both had severely deformed legs, with their feet turned inward and slightly upside down, from untreated clubfoot.

There's a thing I love to do when visiting CURE hospitals: I love to twirl the kids. They line up for it. I grab their wrists, and we spin and spin until I can't stand up anymore. It's a gigglefest!

(Excuse me—Microsoft Word is now giving me the red squiggly line telling me *gigglefest* isn't a word. How am I supposed to write a serious theological work about global health care and CURE without *gigglefest*? I'm using it anyway.)

Anyway, back to this *gigglefest* . . . Before the sun went down, it was Elizabeth who wanted to be twirled over and over. What a sweetheart. She struggled to walk but played so hard. Twirl a giggling kid a long time, and you learn: (1) it's never enough for them and you'll have to tap out from dizziness, and (2) you'll probably remember that kid.

I remember Elizabeth.

CURE gives access to surgeries these kids might never have

otherwise. Parents sometimes give up hope that their kids can ever be healed, only to find out about a CURE hospital, sometimes hundreds of miles away, that will do the surgery and charge exactly $0.00. So these hospitals are busy and special places. I consider them embassies of the kingdom of heaven.

When I visit one of these hospitals, I usually sit in to observe a surgery or two. In Zambia, they do ten to fifteen surgeries each day. Later in my weeklong stay, I came in midafternoon and observed Dr. Moyo preparing as the techs readied the now sleeping little patient. I could see only two feet sticking out from beneath the sheet. I asked him the child's name and for a little background.

"It's a girl. This is the first of two surgeries for this patient. Her name is . . ." He checked. "Elizabeth."

Now, I'm not an emotional man. I promise you that. Not particularly. Not usually. And I know I have a rep to keep. I'm very self-aware and know that people see me as some kind of rugged, resilient American hero. Now, *am* I some kind of hero? I don't know. That's not for me to say. But yeah, probably, but that's not the point here. I don't know why this got brought up. It's embarrassing, this hero talk.

Anyway, when Dr. Moyo and the nurses started praying over her, I got emotional. Her life was about to change drastically.

Dr. Moyo paused before the surgery and told me what Elizabeth's life would have been like if she hadn't been taken to CURE. "She would always be pushed aside. Her disability would forever be her identity. She would always be considered a curse," he said. "She would be everybody's victim."

Everybody's victim? This little girl?

Not happening. Not now. This kid is going to be able to run and play and dance. I'll bet she'll be fast too.

I once met a little girl in Kenya named Ellen who got similar treatment. Her mom couldn't stop smiling, because it wasn't long before Ellen was a complete blur on the soccer field, even at age six. I saw her in action, running circles around boys several years older than her. Even they were laughing at the pure speed of the kid.

No one runs with more unbridled, glorious vivacity than a little kid who's been only sitting and watching her whole life. She wants to be out there with everybody else *so bad* . . . and then she's gets the green light and she's Usain Bolt circa 2012. She can't be stopped.

Sure, other miracles might be impressive, but healing? It changes everything. It's not just another thing. It's a harbinger of what's to come. You've heard of blasts from the past? Healing is a blast from the future.

So much of what we see in the news is about destroying the young: abuse and murders and wars and mass shootings. When horrible things happen, some folks respond with a question for those of us who somehow still believe in a good, all-powerful God: "Where's your God now?"

It's a fair question. But I have a fair answer because God is still at work in the world.

Where's my God now? Go with me to one of these hospitals. I'll show you.

"This is a place where God walks the earth," one lady said. She was smiling. It was at the CURE hospital in Ethiopia, and she was saying it because her life was suddenly changing and a burden was being lifted, literally, off her back.

Where's my God now? Go with me to one of these hospitals. I'll show you.

She was the mom to a boy named Andualem, and while her husband had abandoned her after seeing little Andualem's crooked legs, she wasn't going to give him up. When it came time for him to start his schooling and he couldn't walk with her, she carried him. She put him on her back and walked more than a mile along a dusty road to take him to school.

Every day, there and back, she carried him. She did it for first grade, and then for second grade. Even as he grew bigger and bigger, she carried him. He held her around her shoulders and neck. Fourth grade. Fifth grade. Sixth grade. He grew and grew, and she kept carrying him. Moms are forces of nature.

One day, a truck driver who'd seen her on multiple occasions stopped along the road to talk with her. He mentioned a place where he thought she might be able to find healing for her son. He'd heard of CURE in Addis Ababa.

When she got to the hospital, Andualem's mom showed the staff the scars on her back from carrying her son for so long. And she cried. She found people who cared, and healing for her son. A dream come true.

And that's when she said what she said, about it being a place where God walks the earth, and I can tell you she's right about that.

It's not that the people working in the hospital aren't highly flawed. Of course they are. But that's just it: when humans, such as we all are, want God's kingdom on earth as it is in heaven—when we really catch a vision for it—the reaction from desperate people is "Surely, God is here!"

They know it.

God can use any of us. Jesus said there's an enemy that comes to "steal and kill and destroy." We can see it in the news. It's daily. It's obvious. But He said, "I have come that they may have life, and have it to the full" (John 10:10).

Instead of little bodies being torn apart . . . they are put back together.

The good news of the kingdom is beyond spectacular. I'm glad

I've gotten a taste of it. After all the bizarre, ridiculous, and even horrible things I've been through and seen done in the name of Jesus or religion, I needed this. Being raised in the trauma-filled home of a preacher, and working around Christian entertainment as a radio host, I've seen so much that leaves me asking, "Really, though: What in the world does this have to do with Jesus again? Why are we doing this? Where's the connection? Is this what He told us to do?"

Honestly, that's probably why I am so involved with these hospitals. It's not that there aren't a thousand other great causes. For me, I need to see Jesus at work through His people in a way that so obviously looks just like what He did. I need that. I still need it.

+

One more quick story: I just talked with some nurses who had shown me some photos of Jessica, a sixteen-year-old who'd recently had her cleft palate fixed. After her treatment, they gave her a makeover. The hospital staff and a grandmother brought her back to her village, and her mom was waiting for her. The group arrived, and the mom asked, "Where's Jessica?"

She was standing right there, smiling.

When Jessica's mom realized *this was Jessica*, she hugged her daughter and they both broke down crying out of pure joy.

No wonder people flocked around Jesus. That's a great scene. No wonder people came from all over. They still do when Jesus shows up in us.

This is our future. This is the

promise. All will be made new. Healing is coming. For now, we get mere glimpses, but make no mistake, it's going to happen.

And this is how the world ends: not with a whimper, and not with a bang either.

It ends with a new beginning.

SEVEN

About the Time My Face Hit a Parked Truck

Spiritual doesn't mean solemn, but quite the opposite is true.

Once, as my face was hitting a parked truck (and my face was doing this in front of a large crowd of onlookers), I had an epiphany, as we all would in that situation. Actually, a few epiphanies—simultaneously:

1. I really, truly have no business riding a motorcycle.
2. This is going to make an awesome story if I—you know—am still alive to tell it.
3. What I'm doing here is unquestionably first-rate entertainment for this large crowd of onlookers.

All three were true. It's amazing the sudden clarity you can have in such a fleeting moment. So much reflection.

I'd said no. You should know that. I'd said, "Nah, man, I'm good," several times. But my new friend, a guy I'd met less than an hour earlier, wanted me to have "his" motorcycle.

"Look, I can't take it home," he said. "There are vehicles everywhere here that no one owns. It's a great way to get around Banda." He was a cool surfer dude from San Diego, and we were standing in intense heat in a parking lot in a ruined city on the tip of Sumatra.

Banda Aceh had just been leveled by a tsunami. The guy from San Diego had been there to help recover bodies in the initial days after. I was there because . . . I'd just said yes.

That's it. I'd seen the devastation like everybody else, and I interviewed a guy from a disaster-response group on my radio show who was gathering supplies for survivors who'd lost everything. He asked me if I wanted to go, and after a few moments in thought, I said, "I have no skills—other than puppeteering and playing the accordion—and I don't really see how those things would really help. In a recovery situation."

"But you could use your radio show to raise money to buy supplies," he said, "and we could use another pair of hands to carry stuff." He also mentioned something about how, yes, they would prefer I leave my puppets at home.

"What about my accordi—"

"Look, they've been through a lot already."

My wife liked the idea, and so a few days later, I was off.

It was a brutal flight plan: an hour drive to Fort Lauderdale, then a flight to Dallas, then Los Angeles, Singapore, Medan, and a final leg to Banda Aceh.

I tell you this because, wow, was I tired. And when I got news that I didn't, in fact, have a ticket for that final flight to Banda Aceh, I had no choice but to find a ride. I rode in a dump truck with four Indonesian guys. All of us in the front seat. For thirteen hours.

And they were smoking.

And honking.

Honking like tomorrow would never come and we had only today to honk. As in most of South Asia, honking is a way of life. It's a crowded place, and you don't honk out of anger, you honk to say, "I'm here."

Everybody's honking because everybody's here.

And lo, there was much smoking and honking. Honking and smoking. I was so tired I tried to sleep by hanging my head, golden retriever-style, out the window. This did not work. (Remember the honking part?)

So when we finally arrived, the sun was hot, and I hadn't slept in a very, very long time. My judgment was off. But I was ecstatic to get out of the truck. And while waiting to meet the rest of my team (who had flights), I met the surfer dude from San Diego.

We stood in the parking lot of a hotel that was being used as a staging point for a diverse group of rescue workers. He was showing me "his" motorcycle amid a busy crowd of locals and internationals gathered. Tragically, there were thousands of vehicles that had been abandoned.

"It's really helpful, man. You can just drive it anywhere. It's a great way to get around. You should try it."

I was groggy, but I thought clearly. At least the first time.

"No, I'm good, but thank you."

"Really, just try it . . . It's a great bike," and so forth, he said.

I think I said no a couple of more times but then said something like, "What's the harm, I guess?"

I sat down and did the whole gas-clutch thing out of sequence. I killed the engine. Again and again, I killed it. But I was so tired. I wasn't thinking straight. I now realized my repeated killing of the engine had drawn interest from the crowd.

All of these guys from all of these different countries watching me fail at motorcycling? This hurt. I felt I was representing America poorly. I tried again and again, to defend the honor of the USA, and—*whoa, I just took off!*

Wow, did I take off. I startled myself, leaned back, and immediately launched into a full wheelie as I raced across the lot. Wide-eyed and fully panicking, I shifted my weight forward. Way forward. And hit the brakes too hard.

Next thing I knew, I was going over the handlebars toward an older, red Nissan pickup. This is the part where I had the epiphanies.

As my face collided with the parked truck, I did not lose consciousness. No, I was all too conscious. I was conscious of the truly well-crafted, unforgettable visual I had just provided the crowd. I managed to stand up. They were in disturbed, shocked silence. I tried to make a joke out of it.

"And now, for my next trick . . . ," I said with my finger pointing to the sky.

I don't remember anyone laughing at this joke. I do remember losing consciousness after I finished the joke and collapsing onto the hot gravel parking lot. I remember then thinking I was back in the bean fields of Illinois, where I used to work every summer, and I was walking in the very, very hot sun. Why was the sun so bright today? And who are all of these male voices saying things in other languages? Why is one angry?

When I came to, I was lying on my back, hovered over by many.

They were talking and exclaiming and probably making jokes, but there was also a very kind Australian nurse helping me.

And the angry voice I heard? That was the guy who owned the truck. He was mad about the dent I'd made . . . with my face.

✦

I took a couple of days to recover, but thankfully I hadn't broken anything. I had to pay the red-truck guy $250 to let it go. I guess I understand his frustration. Nobody buys a truck hoping some nerd will come from afar to ram himself into it at high speed. That's no one's dream for their truck, and it was a nice truck. And I'm still sorry.

We didn't stay at that hotel for long. We went to a rural area to help people. But before leaving the country, we had to stop back at the hotel to drop some people off. I hung out briefly outside. Some Indonesian guys saw me, started laughing, pantomimed gunning an accelerator, and said, "Vroom! Vroom! Vroom!"

I respect that. That's legit humor. Slapstick transcends all boundaries.

I really don't mind being made fun of. I'm serious. (I mean, I wrote *Unoffendable*, so I'm kind of asking for it.) You may not think that's possible, but it's likely that you haven't failed as regularly, or as publicly and spectacularly, as I have. Or maybe I'm just weird. Maybe all of these things.

I also suspect it's because I've grown up some. Everyone's impressions of me used to matter so much to me. That is, until I gave up on looking cool. "Cool" wasn't working out for me, anyway.

There's freedom in being uncool. But there's also a risk: people will enjoy you more when you don't mind being uncool, and that makes you cool again. It's the Coolness Paradox, and it's probably best to just not think about it.

In related news, I've never ridden a motorcycle again. "Why,

Brant?" you may sneer. "Are you too *scared*?" And my reply is yes, in fact, I am too scared. That is correct.

Plus, I think firing across a parking lot and smashing into a stationary truck in Indonesia is a pretty spectacular final ride. I can't top that.

I don't want to top that.

+

There's something I've noticed about people I consider spiritually mature, something I admire: they can, and do, laugh at themselves a lot. I want to be like that.

We tend to think of spiritual stuff as solemn stuff. But the most spiritual people, the most Jesus-driven people, I've run across sure laugh easily and much.

I think it's because if we really mature and become more Jesus-like, we become more childlike, and we begin to really know some things: We know we're not in control of the world. We know we're important to our Creator, but we also know we're small.

We know we can't control anything, including everyone's perceptions of us. But we can know what God thinks of us. There's that sense of well-being again.

And, oh yes, we know suffering and hurt are part of life. We feel it too. But as I mentioned earlier, we know how this all ends! It's a party at Dad's house.

He's the Dad we always wanted, and He's throwing a wedding bash. Everyone's invited, and there will be a long, messy line on our way in, some of us limping and others crawling. But inside, the sick find healing. All is made new.

> We tend to think of spiritual stuff as solemn stuff. But the most spiritual people, the most Jesus-driven people, I've run across sure laugh easily and much.

I don't think it'll be very solemn. Bob Dylan described his idea of heaven as "echoes of laughter" (at least I think that was what he was saying?). I think that's right on.

God's kingdom, in its fullness, will involve much, much laughter.

So I vote we start now.

EIGHT

Success Tip:
Embrace the Awkward

Much anxiety is caused by the need to manage perceptions.

Fact: when it comes to living a joyful life, those who are willing to embrace their own awkwardness have a huge advantage.

You know what narcissists absolutely cannot do? Laugh at themselves. They take themselves with a truly grave seriousness. That's a miserable way to live. Oh, they can surround themselves with the trappings of fun. They can post photos of themselves in fun locations. They just can't, you know, really have fun.

I don't want to be like that. And no one around me wants me to be like that. Sometimes, when I'm taking myself too seriously and I start getting anxious about how I'll be perceived by other people, I remember that the stakes aren't as high as I think they are. It's just not about me, ultimately.

I have to remember who I am. In fact, the most famous song about personal peace in the history of the world starts with this very reality. "The LORD is my shepherd," David wrote in Psalm 23. Well, there you have it:

1. I, Brant Hansen, am a sheep, and
2. I have the best Shepherd. I'm safe. I've got what I need.

The next sentence David wrote was "I lack nothing." That puts it in perspective from the get-go.

A good part of loving people is about our own willingness to be awkward. To serve people is to make yourself vulnerable. To interact with other humans is risky. To put your heart into anything is to face exposure.

But if we know the Big Picture, that we have ultimately nothing to fear, that we lack nothing? That's the biggest advantage of all. We're playing with house money.

There was a German exchange student who came to our little town when I was in high school, and he was hilarious. He wasn't a jerk to anyone, but he was spontaneous and unafraid that people might think he was a complete goofball. He told me, in his heavy accent, "I'll never see these people again, so what does it matter?"

> To serve people is to make yourself vulnerable.

There's something very freeing about lowering the stakes. So what if they don't like me? I'm going to try to love my neighbors anyway. I have better conversations now with people because I *know* it's going to be awkward. I *expect* it. Instead of completely avoiding interactions, I go for it. I bring it on.

Love for others can prompt some people to move out of the country or make some other great sacrifice. For me? I'm willing to look goofy. It's a risk I must take, and it gets easier.

At the CURE hospital in Niger, there's always a Thursday afternoon dance party in the kids' activity room. The staff turns on some fun music, and the kids dance. Some dance on crutches; others use canes. Some sit in wheelchairs and dance. Some love to join the dance by being picked up and held.

When adults visit, they might see the kids dance, and think, *That's really neat!* and they watch. But I don't think that's really neat.

No. I think, *Unleash me and my moves!*

My friends know I'm an introvert, but they also know I'm a complete animal on the dance floor. I bring the fire. I will do the robot, the sprinkler, the shopping cart . . . all of them. And then I will fuse the styles. And while fusing the styles, I further fuse that fusion with, say, Cossack folk dance and then perhaps self-defense moves taught by the Israeli military.

"But what happens when they play a slow song?" you ask.

I do all the same moves. Just slower.

People watch me and think I'm strange, but I see the way they look at me. They wish they could be me, having this much fun and laughing this much with the kids. At least that's what I'm telling myself.

Being willing to look goofy is freeing. And it completely fits a faith that is founded on humility and trust and childlikeness and a willingness to be uncool. You know when our faith does look genuinely cringey? When we try to make it cool.

You know when our faith does look genuinely cringey? When we try to make it cool.

An example? I give you Cool Christian Pants.

I know they make them, because I found them advertised, these high-fashion Christian Pants. They even subtly say "Jesus" on them. I'm not making this up. They're eighty-five dollars. This isn't cheap-panted grace.

It did make me think: *How can I know, with complete assurance, that my own current pants are Christian Pants?* The Bible is largely silent on the subject of my pants.

I don't believe my pants have ever made a decision regarding the Lord one way or the other, to be honest. Over the years, my pants have certainly had opportunity, at various church events, to respond and come forward. Only one pair—from Sears—ever did it, during a rendition of "Just As I Am" at church camp. But in retrospect, I have to wonder: *Did the pants come forward just because I was doing it too?*

In truth, I don't know where any of my pants stand. Or the ultimate destination of my previous pants. Except for my parachute pants from high school, which are unquestionably in hell. But the others, I have no idea and don't think about it much.

Seriously, trying to make following Jesus cool never, ever makes sense. Coolness is a trap. Coolness doesn't speak to our deepest need. Coolness doesn't free us. Coolness isn't what people even really want.

Here's a secret I learned from doing radio: People starting in the field think, *I want to be a slick radio host*, but no one actually *likes* slick radio hosts. They want to hear actual humans, not someone trying to sound cool on a microphone.

You have a great voice? Neat. That matters! . . . for about five seconds. You have a terrible voice? No worries. That also matters for about five seconds. Listeners want real, unsmooth humans.[1] This is because what they really want are *friends*. We all do.

---

1. You know those old radio contests? "Be the seventh caller and you will win tickets to the big concert next week" and others like that? I also realized no one cares about those. So I started saying, "The fifty-seventh caller will get a bag of gravel!" and *more* people would call. "Call now and you will be in a drawing for a piece of toast. I will mail it to you," and we're flooded with calls.

People just want real. When you give up trying to be impressive, you can finally speak into someone's life as a friend. The show's over, and real life is happening.

If you're game for this, here are some tips for embracing the awkward lifestyle:

1. Say yes to stuff, knowing you very well might look dumb. At the time of this writing, I was just asked to be on *Good Morning America*. I don't know how that's going to go, but I'm not nervous about it. It might be a disaster. And that's okay.

2. Use the word *experiment* a lot. Maybe you're starting a neighborhood book club, but you're worried it won't continue for more than a few weeks, or maybe no one will be interested. Just tell neighbors it's an experiment. Lowers the stakes.

3. If you do spectacularly fail in front of thousands, don't just own it. *Lean into it.* I saw UFC legend Conor McGregor throw out the first pitch at a Major League Baseball game. It was horrific. He threw it way over everybody on the field and it hit the back wall, near the on-deck circle. When asked about it, he said, "It's the most devastating first pitch ever seen in the iconic Wrigley Field!" But wasn't it terribly offline? He responded, "Well, the venom is there! The power is there . . . but I'm happy with that!"[1] It made me laugh out loud, and it came off as completely likable.

Remember, you don't have to care about what people think of you if you're someone who trusts God. You *do* need to care about what they think of God.

Seeing Him work in the life of someone who isn't otherwise impressive? That makes Him look really, really good.

If *I'm* awesome, well, I get the credit. But if I'm an obviously

> You don't have to care about what people think of you if you're someone who trusts God. You *do* need to care about what they think of God.

flawed human and God does something awesome through me? He gets the credit. That's a wonderful thing.

Smooth is overrated. Oh, people might admire you, but admiration is a fleeting thing. It's a heavy thing too. I used to want admiration, sure. These days? I'd rather skip right past the admiration part to the friend part.

Deep friendships are formed around vulnerability. There's no way around it. It's one thing to share an interest. But when somebody shares a weakness, when someone's willing to be awkward, well . . . now we're talking. The real fun can start.

NINE

I'd Like to Thank the Good Lord. And Also Butch.

God puts even our wounds to work.

For some of us, awkwardness comes more easily than it does to others. I pity those who have to work at it. Me? I'm a natural.

Awkwardness usually peaks in middle or high school, but I like to think I'm still peaking. I do think I felt the awkwardness acutely in high school while I was trying to attract a girl—any girl at all, really—to be my girlfriend.

I did not succeed in this quest. I did, however, have two (2) dates.

I went on a double date to the prom in Casey, Illinois. My date, Marly, was a very nice girl. I was nervous about it but proud of myself that I remembered to get her one of those wrist-corsage things from the florist. The florist asked me, "What kind of flowers?" I could think of only one kind. "Daisies?"

When I handed the wrist-corsage thing made of daisies to Marly, she was very kind and quietly smiled, so that was very nice.

I don't think she had a good time at the prom, though. I think it was because I was stone silent the entire evening. I couldn't think of anything to say. In retrospect, I can see how sitting silently with me at the table for two hours wasn't a fulfillment of her prom dreams.

The next day, we had planned a picnic with our friends. My friend Brian and I drove to the state park, and the girls were there. After a while it seemed to me like Marly was bored with me and a little angry, maybe. I wasn't sure.

But she asked me to play catch with a softball! We grabbed our mitts. And then she had another idea.

"Let's play burnout!" she said.

I furrowed my eyebrows. "Really?"

"Yes. Why not? Don't think you can play with a girl?"

Now, you might know that burnout is a high-IQ game where you throw the ball as hard as you can at the other person to see if they can catch it. This request for burnout caught me by surprise.

"I just . . . I don't know . . . ," I said. "I don't want to play that."

We kept playing catch, and she kept zipping the ball at me. Harder and harder. I kept lobbing my throws back. Even though I wasn't a good athlete, there was one thing I could do pretty well: I could throw hard.

"Come on," she said.

"I'm not going to do that," I said, once again.

Yes, Casey High School had the state champion girls' softball team. They were very proud of this. But still.

"Are you a sexist? You don't think girls can do this as well as you? That's kind of chauvinistic." Marly said this and then zinged the ball back at my face.

I was able to catch it.

"Seriously? I just . . . I'm afraid I'll hurt you. I can throw hard. This doesn't seem like a good idea."

Honestly, I think I told her no at least ten times, but then I gave in.

"Okay, fine. I will play burnout with you. Whatever."

I threw the ball at Marly. Pretty darn hard. Not all-out hard, but pretty hard.

You should know: there's an alarming *thump* a softball makes when it hits the human clavicle. It's the kind of sound you remember for a while.

I remember apologizing profusely and Marly forgiving me. "No, no problem. I asked for it. Not your fault," she said as we all gathered ice from the cooler.

Her dad, it turned out, apparently did see it as my fault. I never actually saw Marly again. We talked on the phone a few weeks later, though, and she was nice. She said something about how her shoulder was recovering and she'd been in a sling for some time.

So that was my prom date.

I'm not Mr. Romance, but I do feel like I did a pretty good job, all things considered. At least she got some free daisies out of it.

✦

Then there was the other date.

My brother, then in college, had a part-time youth-minister job down the road in Shelbyville, Illinois. Everyone liked him. In his youth group was a quiet, sweet girl named Stephanie, whom I eventually and fumble-y asked to the Sweetheart Dance. She said yes, probably because I was Darin's brother. But I was excited about this.

I was to pick her up in my '81 Ford Mustang, which might sound kind of cool, but it was from one of those years when Ford said to themselves, "Let's shake things up and start making Mustangs that are stupid."

Anyway, she gave me very specific directions to her house over the phone. We didn't have smartphones then. So I paid close attention.

"Take Route 130 into town. Turn left at the Shell station, then look for Seventh Street. Turn right on Seventh Street and follow it all the way out of town into the country. As soon as you cross over the railroad tracks, go to the second stop sign and turn right. Follow that three miles and on the left you will see a two-story, green house. That's us."

I hadn't met her family yet, but I knew making a very good impression started with being on time.

I followed the instructions perfectly, drove into the country, second stop sign, turned right, followed it three miles . . . and sure enough, there's the green house, all lit up. As I pulled into the drive-way, I could see a silhouette upstairs, looking out of the window, and then moving away. The outdoor lights were on and welcoming.

I went to the door, rang the doorbell, and almost immediately her mom opened the door.

"Hi! How are you?" she said. "Glad you're here. I think it'll be just a minute!"

I could see Stephanie's father in the living room. He looked at me and seemed a little gruff and intimidating, but he nodded and went back to watching TV.

I waited in the entryway with Mom near the base of the stairs. She asked me if their place was easy enough to find, and I said yes, no problem.

There was a brief, awkward silence, and she said, "Hang on . . . not sure what's taking so long." She looked up the stairs and called out.

"Butch! Come on, Butch, hurry up!"

Uh . . . "Butch"?

"Butch should be down in just a second."

Wait: "Butch"? Does Stephanie have a brother I'm supposed to meet or someth—

At that moment, Butch came bounding down the stairs. And then he stopped. He stared at me, confused. Even frightened.

I stared at him, confused. Even frightened. What the heck was going on?

"Who is *this*?" he said.

"What?" his mom said, and she turned to me. "Who *are* you?"

"I'm . . . Brant. Brant Hansen. I didn't come to pick up Butch. I just—"

Her demeanor turned ice-cold toward me, Brant Hansen, would-be-suitor-turned-home-invader.

"I think you need to leave."

By this time, Dad had gotten up and joined us. He looked threatening.

I said, "Yes . . . I . . . I need to leave. I'm so sorry. Wrong house . . ." I hurried back into the cold night to get into my car and get out of there as quickly as possible.

And that's when it got worse.

I turned the key—nothing. Not a thing. The car was just dark. Something electrical was going on, there was no way I could fix it, of course, and . . . *I'm blocking their garage.* You've got to be kidding. *Now what the heck do I do?*

I had no choice. I had to go back out into the cold, walk up to the door, and ring the doorbell again.

They were greatly displeased to see me again so soon.

I tried to explain. I was trying to pick up Stephanie Davis, and I thought she lived here, and now my car is blocking your garage, and I'm so sorry, and could I use your phone? They somehow didn't seem to know who Stephanie was, which baffled me.

I went into Butch's family's kitchen to use the phone to call Stephanie. Butch's dad was irked. I told Stephanie what was happening. She said her dad and brother would be there in about twenty minutes to work on the car.

And so they were. Meantime, Butch's ride arrived, some guy from his high school who was taking him to a basketball game. Butch's friend knew some stuff about cars, so he and Butch joined Stephanie's dad and brother with flashlights and tools and stuff. Butch's dad even helped out, begrudgingly. Sometimes an '81 Mustang takes a village.

It took a long time, but it seemed like the guys kind of enjoyed it. They figured it out and started up the car and high-fived and laughed and stuff.

I said goodbye to Butch and his mom, the lady I formerly thought was Stephanie's mom, and Butch's friend, and tried to explain to Mr. Davis how his daughter's date wound up with a dead car at some other house in the country.

It was now a little too late to go to the dance, but I was fine with that, and Stephanie was polite about it, and I'm not making any of this up but, wow, do I wish I was.

✦

So those were my two dates. If you have any questions about romance, please email me at mrsmooth@branthansen.com.

Seriously, younger guys sometimes ask me for advice for dating, finding the right woman, et cetera, and you can perhaps see why I don't have much. Advice? No. I have only flashbacks.

I can tell them this: God has had mercy on me. I did manage to talk to a girl in college, and (as I wrote in *Blessed Are the Misfits*) we didn't date. We were pals, and then while studying one night I blurted out, "I love you." She replied with a pause and then, "Uh . . . thanks?" We've been married thirty-three years now.

Thornton Wilder wrote a very short play about two men among the "sick, the blind, and the malformed" who wished to be healed at a pool that was occasionally stirred by an angel. One was a desperate man who had been at the pool for a long time, waiting. The other was a newcomer, a doctor who had been a faithful help to people for a long time and wanted to be healed of a long-standing condition himself.

But the angel appeared and offered healing only for the first man. The doctor objected. "Think," he said, "what I might yet do in Love's service were I but free of this bondage."

And that's when the angel said this:

Without your wound where would your power be? It is your very remorse that makes your low voice tremble into the hearts of men. The very angels themselves cannot persuade the wretched and blundering children on earth as can one human being broken on the wheels of living. In Love's service only the wounded soldiers can serve.[1]

I think there are things that can happen in our lives—ridiculous things, like in this chapter, and far more traumatic things—of which we can say, "I never, ever want to relive that!" and yet still be thankful for them.

Not everyone will understand how that can be. But I think I can better understand Romans 8:28 now, where it says we know that in "all things God works for the good of those who love him," because I can see the good now.

It takes time. And the good doesn't have to outweigh the bad, emotionally. It just means God is at work, redeeming things and untwisting things and unscrambling things, putting our stories to work.

He puts our wounds to work.

It's how He does things. It's His MO. It's how His kingdom works. Everything that's submitted to Him is useful to Him. I thank Him for that.

And, Butch, if you're reading this, thanks for pitching in.

TEN

Jesus' Favorite Subject

There's something we're all yearning for . . . and it's about to happen.

So let's talk about this "kingdom of God" thing. It's a phrase that freaks people out ("Is this a political or theocratic thing?"), but it's also perhaps one of the rare terms that can be simultaneously alarming to some while being incredibly boring to others.

For a lot of church people, the kingdom of God is a topic that doesn't move the emotional needle. I think I understand why. I've noticed religious talk can become like wallpaper to me if it seems like it doesn't relate to my daily life.

So what is it? The kingdom of God is wherever the things God wants to get done get done.

When Jesus taught us how to pray, He told us to ask for more of it. "Your kingdom come, your will be done, on earth as it is in heaven" (Matthew 6:10).

We all have our own kingdoms. And sure, your kingdom, or my kingdom, might be a small sphere of influence, but we all have one. The kingdom of God that Jesus described is stunning, surprisingly subtle, and the exact opposite of boring. It's life-giving.

I think when we really get it, we go from being freaked out or bored by it to loving to talk about it. Jesus sure enjoyed it. In fact, it was Jesus' favorite subject.

I tried to make this point when I was a guest speaker for a big gathering of high schoolers and faculty in a Christian school gym. In retrospect, I don't think I did it very well. In retrospect, I see that perhaps I shouldn't have said what I said quite the way I said it. Yes, in retrospect, I can see clearly now.

I asked them, "So what was Jesus' favorite subject? What did He talk about more than anything else?"

Some brave kids hazarded some good guesses. "Love?" "Oppression?" "Hypocrisy?" "Money?" "Hell?"

Nope. Nope. Nope. Nope. Nope.

"Wait: Nobody knows Jesus' favorite subject that He talked about all the time?" I asked. And then I said that thing I maybe shouldn't have said, now that I think about it: "What kind of 'Christian' school is this?"

In the ol' rearview mirror, I probably shouldn't have said that. Hindsight is 20/20, et cetera. I meant it as a joke, but . . . yeah . . . they were real nice people, I'm sure. Sorry I said that thing I said. My sense of humor is dry and odd. And the bluntness? I'm not above blaming the Asperger's. In fact, I think I'll do that right now: it was totally the Asperger's.

But even though I didn't say it quite right, and even though they never asked me back, it really *is* true: the kingdom of God really was what Jesus was here to tell us about. He said that's why He was sent, to "proclaim the good news of the kingdom of God" (Luke 4:43). But few seem to know it.

Jesus kept trying to explain it to us. Over and over. He unpacked it by telling stories about it and comparing it to things we can understand.

The kingdom of God is like a mustard seed . . .

The kingdom of God is like a pearl . . .

It's like a man who holds a wedding feast . . .

It's like some yeast that a woman took to mix with some flour . . .

He was not just giving us dry theological concepts. He was describing something, something worth giving everything for. It's something worth falling in love with.

For Jesus, "The kingdom is here!" isn't just good news. It's *the* good news. It's the gospel. It's the whole point, and it's a point I'm afraid we're missing.

For Jesus, "The kingdom is here!" isn't just good news. It's *the* good news.

If you zoom in from above on the dusty city of Niamey, Niger, you can see something remarkable.

It's a huge field, maybe a square mile or two, that is nothing but a smoldering trash heap. That's it. It looks like a scar from the sky. But a corner of that trash heap has been walled off. And you can see now that inside the walls it's clean. It's green. Things are growing. Flowers and trees and grass.

You'll see walkways and gardens and several buildings, and in one of the rooms in one of those buildings, if you peer under the roof on a Thursday, well . . . that's where the kids' dance party is happening.

Inside the walls of the CURE hospital complex there, things just . . . thrive. Vulnerable things, like little flowers, and little children who were once told they're trash but are now inside the gate.

When you walk onto the grounds, you are walking from chaos to order, and from devastation to beauty.

Niger is largely a desert country in West Africa. It's dusty and hot (the Apple Weather app will sometimes describe conditions in Niamey not as sunny or partly cloudy but just with the word "dust"), and it's a very tough place to live, let alone be a child with a disability.

But here in the CURE complex? The flowers pop, and employees and locals grow vegetables in the gardens for their families. Kids and their moms wear the brightest colors, and the soundscape is music and laughter.

Kids are given life-changing surgeries and told they're loved by God. If you believe in this kingdom of God—and I sure do—well, here you go. This is what it looks like.

On earth, as it is in heaven.

When God is in charge, healing happens. Chaos turns to beauty. A field of trash and ashes is reclaimed, and it becomes a place for the rejected and broken to dance.

This kingdom is really, really good, and here's my theory: we *all* want it, deep down, even people who won't admit it and don't even believe in it. And here's another of my weird theories—one indicated by goose bumps: we all get brief flashes of it in life, fleeting impressions that leave us moved or yearning for more. We may not even be able to explain why. There's a German word for this, because they have a word for everything: It's *fernweh*, which literally means "farsickness."[1] It's feeling homesick for a place you've never been.

> We *all* want this kingdom, deep down, even people who won't admit it and don't even believe in it.

C. S. Lewis wrote about this desire for our own "far-off country." He said he even felt shy talking about it, because it's so deep within us it seems like we shouldn't even name it. We're not quite sure what the yearning means, or where it came from. We might be a little embarrassed by it.

But for some reason, he wrote, we do have this longing for something that's never actually happened to us. It's not enough to just relive something beautiful we've encountered in the past.

> The books or the music in which we thought the beauty was located will betray us if we trust to them; it was not *in* them, it only came *through* them, and what came through them was longing. These things—the beauty, the memory of our own past—are good images of what we really desire; but if they are mistaken for the thing itself, they turn into dumb idols, breaking the hearts of their worshippers. For they are not the thing itself; they are only the scent of a flower we have not found, the echo of a tune we have not heard, news from a country we have never yet visited.[2]

When a writer for *Atlas Obscura* asked readers what places evoke this sense of farsickness, a lot of people mentioned Irish coastlines or the highlands of Scotland. But many others responded with poetry, or fictional places like Lewis's Narnia or Tolkien's Middle-earth.[3] (I would go with the Shire. I don't even have to think about it. But that's me.)

Good filmmakers, I believe, know exactly how to tap into this. They can combine sound and image to evoke this nostalgia for places we've not been. We tear up. We get goose bumps.

I believe this is part of our longing for our real home. It's the kingdom of God, where every tear is wiped away from our eyes. Where things are finally set right. Where everything sad becomes untrue. Where reunions happen.

We all want to go back to Eden. Even if our minds deny the idea of Eden, our souls simply can't. Our souls are hungry for the kingdom, to get back to the way things ought to be. Based on my observations, I'd say we humans are even obsessed with it.

We physically react to it.

Here's a small example: I'm not a particularly emotional guy. I'm a little robotic. But show me one of those videos where a dad or mom returns from serving in the military and surprises a little girl or boy and . . . I can't handle it. I recently saw one where Dad snuck into a classroom in his fatigues, and when his daughter opened her eyes, he was right there. She didn't immediately hug him. She just sobbed and sobbed, overwhelmed and overjoyed, before finally throwing herself, limp, into his arms.

I almost can't type now. Gets me every time.

It doesn't even have to be a kid. Have you seen the "soldier reunited with dog" videos? The car door opens and the dog comes bounding out of the house in a tail-wagging frenzy? Yeah. I can't handle those either. It's too good.

Imagine that . . . multiplied. The kingdom of God in its fullness, when people are reunited with those who have gone before. Once lost to us but now found. Together again. We all long for it.

People around the world watch the Olympics opening and closing ceremonies. They see the nations walking in peace and a massive, diverse crowd joyfully celebrating. And all over the world, people get goose bumps.

When I was a kid, I watched our Olympic hockey team beat the Russians. It was an upset no one saw coming. Just a bunch of scrappy college kids, amateurs, against Russian pros. The crowd went wild. Everyone was in tears. We love upsets, and not just for our favorite teams. People love Cinderella stories in the NCAA basketball tournament each March.

When the impossible happens, the underdog wins? Goose

bumps. There's something about the last suddenly being elevated to first. The world turns upside down, which we intuit is really right side up. It's another theme of the kingdom of God. The humble are exalted.

There's another sign there, I think, pointing to the place we're nostalgic for.

I recently saw a video of a girl being able to hear for the first time. Shock. Laughter. Tears. And again: goose bumps. There's just something about healing and restoration. As I say, healing is an advance trailer of heaven, and so, I believe, are these other goose-bump moments. Just little glimpses ahead.

"The kingdom is here," Jesus said. And then He reached out . . . and people were healed. Life was set right. The way they were supposed to be. The way they were always supposed to be.

We can all feel it.

ELEVEN

Party Practice

Because God, Himself, is joyful.

Since Jesus described the kingdom as a big party, I think we should practice up.

Some people don't know how to enjoy a good party. They're too worried about themselves, or they're too bitter or anxious. I understand all of that.

Maybe that's another reason Jesus said we won't be able to enter the party unless we become like children. Little kids know how to do this. They're not particularly concerned with looking good, posing with the right people, trying to impress somebody with status, or getting some selfies for social media.

Kids don't need a shot of something to feel alive for a little while.

They know how to have fun. They just want to know where the games and cupcakes are. They don't mess around. They don't have to be cool.

They come by this humility naturally. Look, they know they're dependent. There's no hiding it. Think about it: If someone has to drive you everywhere, or feed you, or pick out your clothes because you can't quite do it "right"? You're either a mega-celeb, or a kid.

But kids have way more fun than celebs. Celebs simply must constantly be doing something novel, wearing something no one else is wearing, or reinventing themselves. Kids? They're more than cool with the same simple thing! Over and over and over! I love how G. K. Chesterton described it:

> Because children have abounding vitality, because they are in spirit fierce and free, therefore they want things repeated and unchanged. They always say, "Do it again"; and the grown-up person does it again until he is nearly dead. For grown-up people are not strong enough to exult in monotony. But perhaps God is strong enough to exult in monotony. It is possible that God says every morning, "Do it again" to the sun; and every evening, "Do it again" to the moon. It may not be automatic necessity that makes all daisies alike; it may be that God makes every daisy separately, but has never got tired of making them. It may be that He has the eternal appetite of infancy; for we have sinned and grown old, and our Father is younger than we.[1]

Exactly. But people don't usually think about God this way. Ask people to describe the god they believe in, and they might say theological-sounding stuff: "God? He's omniscient, omnipresent, and omnipotent." They rarely add, "And He totally knows how to have a good time."

We don't think of Him that way. But He is a joyful being, and more so than anyone you know.

In Genesis 1, God clearly got a kick out of creating. Especially creating us! He saw that it was "good" at every stage—except, that is, when He created a human person. That was even better. That was "*very* good."

So, in the Bible, the story begins in joy and delight. And how does it end? With one heck of a party.

The God of the Bible is not the Big Angry Sheriff of the Sky who's worried about things. No, He's having a good time. Even now. He's not worried one bit.

He's the Biggest Party Host in the universe.

> In the Bible, the story begins in joy and delight. And how does it end? With one heck of a party.

When Carolyn and I got married, we certainly had no idea how to throw a fun party. Our wedding reception featured some long folding tables with dishes that had nuts and mints. That's it. And the mints weren't even Junior Mints. They were those little square, powdery ones that no one likes. People just sat quietly, and that was the whole "party."

I'm cringing even now. But I will let it go. I promise, the wedding feast of the Lamb described in the New Testament will be way more fun than that.

If you know anything about wedding parties in traditional cultures, they are not brief, tame events. They're usually raucous and fun for everybody. In other good news, I just did a thorough Bible search, and the phrase "powdery mints" is nowhere to be found.

Another thing about this epic party: not everyone wants to be there. Not surprising, I guess, because people turn down good things all the time. Jesus told stories about a rich man or a king throwing parties and all the VIPs turning them down. They made up excuses. Maybe they thought they were too good for it.

NO... I don't really KNOW
MUCH ABOUT GOD...
EXCEPT THAT HE's Ticked OFF.

This meant other people got to come, like "the poor, the crippled, the lame, the blind" (Luke 14:13).

The humble are *in*, which means the party is way better. Children and childlike people won't miss the invite. They're not the types to hem and haw over receiving a gift. A six-year-old doesn't get a wonderfully fun toy and say, "Oh, you shouldn't have," or think, *Oh no! I haven't bought anything for this person that's of equal value!*

Nope. That's dumb. They just rip open the box and start playing.

✦

I love these words from the late Mike Yaconelli about how prideful and just plain boring we adults can get. He began by quoting Rabbi Edward Cohn:

Life is tough. It takes up a lot of your time, all your weekends, and what do you get in the end of it? . . . I think that the life cycle is all backward. You should die first, get it out of the way. Then you live twenty years in an old-age home. You get kicked out when you're too young. You get a gold watch, you go to work. You work forty years until you're young enough to enjoy your retirement. You go to college; you party until you're ready for high school; you go to grade school; you become a little kid; you play. You have no responsibilities. You become a little baby; you go back into the womb; you spend your last months floating; and you finish up as a gleam in somebody's eye.

Then Yaconelli continued:

It's hard to imagine we were a gleam in someone's eye once. What happened to the gleam in our eye? What happened to that joyful, crazy, spontaneous, fun-loving spirit we once had? The childlikeness in all of us gets snuffed out over the years.

A. W. Tozer once said, "This society has put out the light in men's souls." He had it right. The more pagan a society becomes, the more boring its people become. The sign that Jesus is in our hearts, the evidence of the truth of the gospel is . . . *we still have a light on in our souls.* . . .

The light in our souls is not some pious somberness. It is the spontaneous, unpredictable love of life. Christians are not just people who live godly lives. We are people who know how to *live* period. Christians are not just examples of moral purity. We are also people filled with a bold mischievousness. Christians not only know how to practice piety. We also know how to party.

I believe it's time for the party to begin.[2]

✦

And so we go back to Niger, to the wildly fun dance parties: I will always remember a group of four teenage girls who were there. They were all victims of a rare virus, one that affects the malnourished. It severely disfigures their faces.

Because of how they looked, they faced utter rejection in each of the villages where they'd lived. They were called names, and they were considered cursed by demons. They spent much of their days hidden away to avoid embarrassment and ridicule.

At the hospital, though, they found one another. They understood one another. They giggled and played and walked together. And they danced too. They could just be girls. They were free. No more hiding. No more shame. They weren't trying to impress anyone either. They just got to play.

And I'm telling you, there's nothing like a dance party of the uncool. No one's trying to be anything. No one can pretend they're fashionable. There's nothing more fun than this kind of scene. There we were: black people, white people; little girls and boys in casts; doctors and nurses and moms and friends. All were jumping and goofing around and making each other laugh. Right there next to a giant trash field in one of the poorest cities in the world.

There was nothing at stake. We were free. Forget *Dancing with the Stars*; this was dancing with our scars, and really, who can find a better party than that?

Some religious people will say, "That's nice, but this sort of childish fun is a frivolous distraction to the real work of the kingdom!" But they're the wrong-iest kind of wrong, and C. S. Lewis totally agreed with me about that. "Dance and game *are* frivolous, unimportant down here; for 'down here' is not their natural place," he wrote. "Here, they are a moment's rest from the life we were placed here to live. But in this world everything is upside down." And then he said something that totally could have been the title of this book: "Joy is the serious business of Heaven."[3]

> There's nothing like a dance party of the uncool.

Right on. So practice up. We're getting ready for the big time.

TWELVE

The Style of God

On the joy of radical hospitality, where the outsiders are insiders.

Joey was one of my favorite neighbors.

Because of my aforementioned awkwardness with other humans, I don't naturally strike up conversations or approach people. But Joey is the opposite of shy. He happily talks to everybody. I love that.

We live in a neighborhood of townhomes that's packed in, but people generally like their privacy. So, for anyone as outgoing as Joey, that's a challenge. It could even be discouraging.

Joey was about thirty years old at the time, and he lived with his parents. He would walk the neighborhood every day using the assistance of a walker. He was born with neurological issues and suffered a traumatic brain injury when he was nineteen. He had to relearn how to speak. Walking and moving about were tough because of his loss of balance.

Nevertheless, he was relentless about talking to people, asking how they're doing, trying to strike up conversations with neighbors. I admired his purehearted moxie. Everyone knew who Joey was, even if most of them didn't know anyone else.

Joey organized weekly "walks for wellness" and invited people to meet him in front of the community center on Saturday mornings. He would post the invite every week, and most of the time I didn't think much of it. But one Saturday, I happened to drive by and saw him waiting outside by himself.

So I thought maybe it would be good to go for a walk for my wellness. I joined him, and off we went. It was slow, for sure, but he played music on his iPhone, and I like music, so I asked about all the artists. He liked to sing along, and I thought that was cool because I like to do that too.

I joined him the next couple of weeks and then asked him if he would come over so we could jam. I play guitar, in addition to the accordion, and we could find some songs he enjoyed singing. He was extremely excited about it.

So that became a thing. He would come over, and we would R-O-C-K in the USA really loud in the little dining area of our town house. He liked classic rock like Tom Petty or the Rolling Stones, and I would look up the chords and we'd just take off.

He also liked scary stuff. Dark, horror-type stuff. His favorite thing was being part of a big haunted-house production at Halloween, and he talked about that a lot. I don't think he entirely knew what to make of the fact that I was a Jesus person. He'd mentioned that he didn't believe in God, and he'd had some bad interactions before with Christians. He also said his parents were not religious. I told him I understood all of that.

Once we figured out how to get his walker in my car, I was able to drive him places.

He really loved to belt out those songs. I'm sure he still does, but the problem is he doesn't live around here anymore.

Joey told me his parents were moving a few hours away, to a retirement community, so he would be going with them. He said he was sad about it because he finally felt like he connected with someone in the neighborhood. I was sad about it too.

We decided to throw a going-away, "Joey Appreciation" party and hoped some people would show up. Balloons, decorations, snacks, the whole deal. Joey was stoked about it and said his parents (whom I still hadn't met yet) were happy that we were going to have a party for him.

We advertised it on our neighborhood social media, and we let people know it was an open house to tell Joey goodbye and "We love you."

We filled the house with the decorations and got a cake and some drinks to put on ice. For the first thirty minutes or so, it was just me, my wife, and Joey. Honestly, I was feeling sad and a little embarrassed, but Joey was fine with it and enjoyed sitting at our table and talking with me and Carolyn surrounded by all the balloons.

Our across-the-street friends showed up, a mom and her girl, and that made it feel a little more like a party for a while. So that was nice.

And then the doorbell rang, and there was a couple we hadn't met before. And then a nearby family with a six-year-old boy who always enjoyed talking to Joey showed up. And then Joey's parents.

Then more people we didn't even know. And then lots of people we didn't know!

Our little house was jammed, with people spilling out into our courtyard. Many neighbors were meeting each other for the first time.

"You see this," I told Joey. "This is because of you. This is how much you mean to this neighborhood, and how much you will be missed."

He told Carolyn and me that he had no idea he was this loved, or that he'd made an impact like that. Joey's parents, too, were very surprised, and they stayed the rest of the evening. They were very, very happy. I was so thankful, too, for everyone who'd shown up. Relieved and thrilled and exhausted.

The next morning, as I walked our dog, I strolled past Joey's townhome. They were on their way out, but they hadn't left just yet, and the front door was open. Joey's mom saw me and came outside.

She told me that the party made her see that Joey had meant a lot to people all this time, and that she was thinking more about God. About how He maybe sees people differently than we do, and even when horrible things happen, some wonderful things might happen too. Maybe that's how God does things.

I told her I think that's *exactly* how God does things. I think He especially draws close to people like Joey. That's His style. And that's why I love Him.

✦

I've learned that parties are a big part of God's style because His style is one of radical hospitality. The best definition I've ever heard for hospitality is "making outsiders feel like insiders."

In the Bible, God repeatedly calls for His people to be distinct by welcoming in the stranger, the orphan, and the widow. This sets His followers apart.

I've heard people say it's why God chose to partner with Abraham, who had issues, for sure, but was fantastically hospitable. It's a running theme with him. It's like God looked around and said, "Now *this* guy: I like the way he operates. I can work with this."

Frederick Buechner wrote a book of his own definitions of things. It's a fun read, called *Wishful Thinking: A Theological ABC.* And when he was explaining what God's glory is, that's exactly what he said: it's God's *style.*

Every great painter or architect or artist of any sort has a style. I was driving through Grand Rapids, Michigan, in a residential neighborhood when I noticed a home and thought, *Wait, is that a Frank Lloyd Wright . . . ?* I looked it up and, sure enough, it was. And I'm not at all learned in architecture. It's just that Frank Lloyd Wright had a style.

Van Gogh, Rembrandt, Monet . . . same thing. Even if you've never heard a particular aria before, and like me you're no expert, you still might be able to listen for just a bit and say, "That's Mozart!"

Here's what Buechner wrote:

In the words of Psalm 19:1, "The heavens are telling the glory of God." It is the same thing. To the connoisseur, not just sunsets and starry nights, but dust storms, rain forests, garter snakes, and the human face are all unmistakably the work of a single hand. Glory is the outward manifestation of that hand in its handiwork just as holiness is the inward. To behold God's glory, to sense God's style, is the closest you can get to God this side of paradise, just as to read *King Lear* is the closest you can get to Shakespeare.[1]

God has an MO, a style, which He uses all the time: He uses the humble. He uses the little things, the seemingly unimpressive, overlooked things to do the marvelous. He enjoys it. He loves real parties with real hospitality, where outsiders are treated like insiders. So I'm honestly trying, in my own halting fashion, to make His style my style.

We also recently threw a party at our house for the team of about a dozen landscapers that comes through our development and mows and trims. They're almost all new immigrants from Guatemala, and I asked their boss if we could provide lunch on a particular day. She was very surprised but eagerly said yes.

He uses the seemingly unimpressive, overlooked things to do the marvelous.

I went and got some pizzas and salads and cookies and drinks, and we set up tables and chairs. It turns out Spotify has a "Guatemala's Top 50" playlist, so I cranked it. I'm bad at Spanish, but we had a lot of laughs, and it was a blast. Plus, I loved seeing the reaction on our neighbors' faces as they drove by. (*Who are the Hansens partying with now? The lawn guys?!*)

We do stuff like this enough that we're now the party house. Imagine that. My natural bent? I'm judgmental. I'm an introvert. I never went to parties in high school. No, I was (for real) the president of the Illinois Student Librarians Association. But you know what? This is fun.

I love what Eugene Peterson wrote about what we should be known for.

> The word *Christian* means different things to different people. To one person it means a stiff, uptight, inflexible way of life, colorless and unbending. To another it means a risky, surprise-filled adventure, lived tiptoe at the edge of expectation. . . . If we get our information from the biblical material, there is no doubt that the Christian life is a dancing, leaping, daring life.[2]

So I'm trying. Yep, it's a risky thing. When we try to love people, we're vulnerable. When we try to throw a party, maybe nobody comes. Maybe we feel dumb.

But I'm convinced God loves when we try. That's just His style.

THIRTEEN

On the Gentle Art of
Freaking People Out

*We're supposed to be so hopeful that
people wonder what's up.*

A question for you: Based on whatever knowledge you have of Jesus, if you could choose only one word to describe Him, what would you choose?

Dallas Willard, a very wise, extraordinarily learned man whom I keep quoting, picked a word that still has me thinking. Of all the words at his disposal, he picked this.

Relaxed.

I'm still mulling that one, but I like it. Jesus really doesn't seem anxious, does He? He's certainly not hurried. He's in the moment. He's not stressing about getting everything done. He's not bothered by deadly storms; we know that—He brings cushions for those.

Relaxed.

So if I believe the things Jesus believes, I will also be relaxed. And you know what? One fun thing about living in a highly anxious, highly hurried society: When you're relaxed, when you don't freak out? It freaks people out.

They don't quite know what to do with it. I think they're drawn to it too. In a world of insecurity, security draws people in. A secure person, whose mind isn't cluttered with hurry and worry, can intently listen.

And listeners are in short supply. We can see that with the overwhelming demand for counseling (which we'll talk about later).

> In a world of insecurity, security draws people in.

If you can focus on someone else, and ask genuinely curious questions, people will wonder what's right with you.

There's this scripture that's been misused (haven't they all?) to smack people over the head with theological arguments. It's where Peter said to "always be prepared to give an answer to everyone," and I've had people tell me that's why I should study stuff—to argue with people and win.

But that misses the entire point of the Scripture, because it goes on, and I'll italicize something here:

Always be prepared to give an answer to everyone who asks you to give the reason for the hope that you have. (1 Peter 3:15)

I also went ahead and underlined it because it's my book and I can do that. (Not the Bible, I mean. This book.) It's like Peter even anticipated people getting the wrong impression, because he continued by telling people to "do this with gentleness and respect."

Think about that: Peter expected us to be so different that

other people actually notice how *hopeful* we are, even in the midst of . . . anything and everything. No matter what, we're hopeful. Not complaining. Not griping. Not going on about how the country is going to hell in a handbasket.[1]

In case we want to say, "Yeah, but we are living in special times. Christians are losing their rights, and there's rampant injustice, and . . . ," it's worth reading the whole letter from Peter. The people he was writing to? They were suffering for their faith. He continually referenced this, knowing what they were going through. He was saying yes, people are going to try to hurt you, but don't be afraid. They'll ask why you're so hopeful, so be ready with a gentle answer.

Hope radiates. We live in a culture almost devoid of it, honestly. I saw a recent study of teen girls in the US that showed nearly three out of five feel sad or hopeless.[1] We've never seen numbers like that. It's heartbreaking. There's a reason we refer to perusing social media as "doomscrolling" instead of "hope-scrolling."

I can't remember who said it, but some comedian pointed out how hilarious the "throw" is on network morning shows to the news anchor. Everyone's smiling, looking great, and it goes something like this:

HOST ROB: And now we check in with Jen for the news.
   Good morning, Jen!
ANCHOR JEN: Good morning, Rob!
TRISH: Good morning, Jen!
ANCHOR JEN: Good morning, Trish! (*Turns to face camera.*) And good morning, everyone! Four hundred people died in a building fire overnight, and . . .

---

1. It just occurred to me that the only time we use the perfectly lovely word *handbasket* is in this context. Just invoke the word and you know exactly where we're going.

They'll tell you "Good morning!" eight times . . . and then immediately tell you why it's not. It all feels pretty hopeless, honestly. Someone with real hope sure seems like an oddball.

Now, you can't talk about hope without at least one reference to *The Shawshank Redemption*. It's an unwritten rule among us big-time authors. It's all about hope, of course, and it has a scene that is still one of my all-time faves.[2]

It's when prisoner Andy commandeers the PA system, and everyone out in the drab, violent, gray prison yard suddenly hears Mozart wafting through the air. Everyone stops. Beauty has broken through!

I feel like we can bring more beauty into the world, more hope. I know it sounds like a cliché, but darn it, it's true: the darker the world gets, the brighter we can shine.

+

Hope isn't the only thing that freaks people out in a wonderful way.

The entire way of life that Jesus gave us is so countercultural, and not just counter to our culture either. I mean, seriously, who *loves* their enemies, for real?

The Sermon on the Mount is profoundly freeing in a thousand ways, but even beyond that, it's also a way of life that leaves people wondering, *Can I really do that? Is that allowed?* Can we truly forgive people? Live without fear? Not worry about anything? Not live in anger? Give people more than they ask for? If forced to go one mile, go an extra one? Turn the other cheek if someone hits you in the face?

This is a strange and awesome way to live. I say we try it. So did Brennan Manning:

---

2.   It's right up there with the "I sail! I'm a sailor!" scene from the equally profound and hope-centered *What About Bob?*

If indeed we [Christ followers] lived a life in imitation of his [Jesus], our witness would be irresistible. If we dared to live beyond our self-concern; if we refused to shrink from being vulnerable; if we took nothing but a compassionate attitude toward the world; if we were a counterculture to our nation's lunatic lust for pride of place, power, and possessions; if we preferred to be faithful rather than successful, the walls of indifference to Jesus Christ would crumble. A handful of us could be ignored by society; but hundreds, thousands, millions of such servants would overwhelm the world. Christians filled with the authenticity, commitment, and generosity of Jesus would be the most spectacular sign in the history of the human race. The call of Jesus is revolutionary. If we implemented it, we would change the world in a few months.[2]

We can do this, you know. It's not impossible to learn to follow Jesus. We can love our enemies. We can learn how to forgive people and live without anger. We can learn more and more how to trust God day-to-day. These are doable things, and they are things that make life more joyful. Peace is at hand—the inner kind that everyone is looking for.

Unfortunately, I'm afraid our church culture has taught us that the Christian life is simply about assenting to a list of truths so that we're "saved." Then we make it about studying things, stockpiling information, and having some God-themed experiences.

> We can do this, you know. It's not impossible to learn to follow Jesus.

But Jesus wants us to *follow* Him. It's way more interesting, dangerous, and, yes, fun. It changes us. We become different people. Please let me remind you that I am, by nature, a brooding, fatalistic nihilist. I'm a different person now.

I'm more relaxed and confident now, and I think it's because of the way God has helped me be more secure. As I learn how to do this loving-others thing, I'm being freed to enjoy others too.

One guy in our neighborhood in midtown Harrisburg, Pennsylvania (we'll call him "Robert"), was a round, older man with a leg problem who would hobble past our house. He talked very loudly, so I initially found him kind of annoying. But it turns out he just couldn't hear well. He was extraordinarily sweet, and also very simple. He had special needs and lived nearby with his brother. Other people in the neighborhood ignored him. I enjoyed him.

He wore a Dallas Cowboys stocking cap. So I, Brant Hansen, longtime awkward introvert who's been mostly all about himself and his insecurities, invited myself over to watch the Cowboys with him.

And so we did. It was a dark little living room, but he had a couch set up about fourteen inches from a giant TV. The reception was not good, so I couldn't always see what was going on, but I seriously didn't really care. We were both happy to watch a game with a friend. I didn't feel any pressure to make conversation or anything.

I think I used to steer clear of guys like Robert because I was afraid I'd be overwhelmed with neediness or something. Turns out Robert was never needy. Sometimes the doorbell would ring and he'd be at the door with a small need, I guess. One time he asked for some Tylenol for a headache. A couple of other times he came by to ask me to please tie his shoes. We went to some minor-league baseball games together.

I enjoyed every minute of this. There was no sacrifice on my part.

After we moved away, I sent a neighbor a Cowboys jacket to give to Robert for his birthday. (I usually don't remember birthdays, so again—baby steps.) I hope he liked it. I'm confident I miss him way more than he misses me. It's weird how love can work that way . . . when I finally try it.

I've learned that spiritual growth isn't about gritting your teeth and forcing yourself to do that thing, or stop doing that other thing, day after day and into forever. That's not it at all. Spiritual growth is about letting God give us a personality makeover, from the inside out.

When that happens, we start doing things more naturally. We don't even have to think about it too much, we just do it. For example, let's say you spend ten minutes just thanking God for things. Then you walk into the coffee place and the baristas are slower than usual, for some unknown reason. Do you think you might be a little more patient? I highly suspect you would.

Spiritual growth is about letting God give us a personality makeover, from the inside out.

We just react differently. The time spent practicing gratitude is like practicing free throws: It allows you to respond, in the pressure of the game, in a way you don't even have to think about. It becomes second nature.

I don't always get it right, but sometimes I do. Like one time, when I was in a hurry and the light turned yellow and then red at the busiest, slowest stoplight in town. I had to stop. I thought, *And now I'm going to be sitting here forev*— and then a car hit mine from behind.

I jumped out instinctively and, highly aggravated, headed back to see the damage. As I did, I saw a young guy getting out of the offending car . . . and wait, was that Jeremy? I knew him from our church. He was sixteen and had just plowed into the back bumper of my "classic" Buick LeSabre.

In a very hopeful sign that I'm changing: I angrily motioned to him and said, "Let's hug."

He was a bit shaken and confused but said, "Sure?" and we hugged it out and I told him, "This is totally going to freak everybody out," and we then shook hands, high-fived, and went back to our cars.

I just liked the idea of a crowd of drivers across several lanes sitting, watching an accident, seeing the drivers emerge shaken and angry, and then suddenly hugging and laughing. I still laugh thinking about it. You don't get opportunities like that all the time.

I'll bet Jeremy still remembers, and that makes me happy. It helps that I'm growing up and learning to relax a bit. It also helps that I was driving an old Buick LeSabre.

FOURTEEN

Earth Is Crammed with Heaven

The joy of being relaxed, dedicated, and aware.

We certainly do have the option to worry about things. We can engage in a lifestyle of worry. There's plenty to worry about, and ample opportunity to do so . . . 24/7, worldwide.

Some people, I gather, are even worried about others not worrying. They think if we don't worry about what they're worried about, maybe we just don't care enough.

But worrying and caring are two very different things. We shouldn't conflate them. Popular author James Clear made this . . . he made this . . . I'm trying not to say "clear" again, but he made this clear: "You can be relaxed and dedicated," he wrote. "Just because you worry more, doesn't mean you care more."[1]

Exactly. Relaxed and dedicated. Jesus is the obvious example: He cares about us more than we can imagine, but He's not freaking out either. There He was at what we now call the Last Supper knowing full well what was about to happen, and He was already talking about the next time He'd have wine with His friends.

He's thinking big picture. Always.

+

I just saw a clip of an ESPN interview with three remarkable athletes. They play for the University of Oklahoma women's softball team, which, at the time of this writing, is as dominant as any team in NCAA sports has ever been. They just won their fifty-third game in a row, and their third consecutive national championship.[2] They're a juggernaut.

So the ESPN reporter asked a fine question. What he got in response had to be a bit of a shock. I was shocked, watching. All three of the young players seated at the press conference proceeded to give a succinct, tag-team master class explaining joy.

The reporter asked about the pressure of the win streak and dominance: "How do you keep the joy for so long when anxiety seems like a thing that could very easily set in?"

Shortstop Grace Lyons answered:

Well, the only way that you can have a joy that doesn't fade away is from the Lord. And any other type of joy is actually happiness that comes from circumstances and outcomes. . . . That's really the only answer to that, because there's no other way that softball can bring you that because of how much failure comes in it, and how much of a roller coaster the game can be.

Center fielder Jayda Coleman then joined in:

One thousand percent agree with Grace Lyons. . . . I think that is what makes our team so strong is that we're not afraid to lose, because it's not the end of the world if we do lose. Yes, obviously, we worked our butts off to be here and we want to win, but it's not the end of the world, because our life is in Christ, and that's all that matters.

Then this, from infielder Alyssa Brito:

You guys see us doing this [points to eyes and then upward], but we're really fixing our eyes on Christ. You can't find a fulfillment in an outcome, whether it's good or bad. And I think that's why we're so steady in what we do. . . .

No matter the outcome, whether we get a trophy in the end or not, this isn't our home, and I think that's what's amazing about it, is we have so much more. We have an eternity of joy with our Father, and I'm so excited about that. And, yes, I live in the moment, but I know this isn't my home, and no matter what, my sisters in Christ will be with me in the end when we're with our King.[3]

Like I said: a master class. Sometimes wisdom wears a softball uniform.

"Relaxed" does not mean you don't put forth effort. "Peaceful" doesn't mean bland. And being focused on the truly long term can help you excel because it removes the intense pressure of the immediate.

Honestly, I watch this on YouTube and I marvel. Not only do I wish I had known that stuff when I was their age, but I'm in awe of their ability to be in the moment and extemporaneously give such brilliant answers when under pressure. It's almost like the pressure doesn't faze them.

Or maybe it's exactly that the pressure doesn't faze them. Not now. Now they can be relaxed.

That's the beauty of the big picture: when it's a picture this beautiful and this rock solid, you don't have to worry about results crushing you. *But what if we lose?* You just keep doing your thing.

+

And that's just it: we do our thing, and we let God do His.

Maybe we're all like that little boy who was in a crowd of thousands who came to see Jesus. He brought his lunch: some bread and some fish. Jesus wound up feeding the entire hungry crowd with it. They even had leftovers.

There's no way the kid thought what he brought would go that far. But that's just it: maybe we bring what we have and then just watch what Jesus can do with it.

Then there's the episode where Jesus raised Lazarus from the dead. Right before He did it, he told the people standing around to roll the stone away, the one blocking the tomb. So they did it, and Jesus then commanded Lazarus to come out.

Maybe we bring what we have and then just watch what Jesus can do with it.

Jesus could have rolled the stone away Himself, of course, but He told others to do it.

My farmer friend Keith told me he thinks it's because we need to learn the lesson: we do what we can do, and then God will do what only He can do. I think Farmer Keith is onto something.

We still get to be part of something wonderful, but we can relax about the outcomes. It's not on us. We don't have to do what we can't do.

+

I DID NOT EXPECT
MY LUNCH TO
GO VIRAL

It turns out there's a lot I can't do.

Not only can I not feed a massive crowd with some kid's sack lunch, but I can barely feed myself. I'm not good at cooking things or even grilling things. I recently messed up something with our gas grill and caused a large, sudden flash of fire. I wasn't hurt bad, but it singed my eyebrows.

There's something disconcerting about the lasting smell of one's own burned eyebrows. But that's not my point here. My point is, I'm not good at grilling. I will not be remembered for that, and I'm cool with it.

I'm not sure it matters if or how I'm recalled, outside my family and friends. I'm a fairly successful (?) radio host, but I don't know if I'll be remembered for that either. I'm guessing this book I'm typing right now isn't going to win a Nobel anything, even though it totally should. That's right, Nobel committee, I'm calling you out right now. Will you have the guts to give me the Prize in Literature, even after I just referenced the smell of my eyebrows?

Seriously: in the end, if or when people remember me, they may just say, "You know what? Now that I think about it, that Brant guy sure played with a lot of kids."

Now *that* I have done, and I've done it everywhere. I didn't plan it, but I'm happy to report the Lord has allowed me to play with kids in Ethiopia and Indonesia and Haiti and Afghanistan and El Salvador. And then there's Senegal, where they schooled me in soccer, and India, where they were amused at my attempt to play cricket. I've gotten to play tag in Rwanda and twirl kids in Thailand.

I've gotten to play, and play with great abandon, with kids in Mexico and Uganda and Peru and Zambia. Kenya, too—epic keep-away games there.

I could go on, but you get the point. I'm so thankful for the memories of giggling kids. But one thing was pretty consistent: In all of these places, I noticed grown men don't play with kids.

It's just not something they typically do in traditional cultures. It's weird to them.

I'm pretty sure Jesus' culture was that way. So I love imagining Him relaxed and playing with kids, and playing all out, laughing and twirling the kids and enjoying them. His disciples would have been scandalized. But He just kept doing it.

They may have been publicly embarrassed. They wanted to take the kids away. No self-respecting, full-grown man, a rabbi no less, would be so undignified, right?

Wrong. This one was different.

Jesus said if you've seen Him you've seen the Father. Imagine that. This is God? This is not normal god behavior. Zeus does not play with little kids. Baal does not play with little kids. Thor does not play with little kids. Allah does not play with little kids.

> Jesus said if you've seen Him you've seen the Father. Imagine that. This is God? This is not normal god behavior.

The God of the Bible? He's all in. He not only defends the little ones, but He enjoys them. He even tells us that if we want to enter His kingdom, we need to be like them.

If the Lord of all creation, the almighty God Himself, who has the world on His shoulders, relaxes and plays with kids, well, I'm pretty sure we should approach life that way too.

This makes me think of an oft-quoted[1] bit from the epic poem *Aurora Leigh* by Elizabeth Barrett Browning:

> Earth's crammed with heaven,
> And every common bush afire with God:

---

1. I say "oft-quoted" even though I just read it for the first time yesterday. I want to sound like I'm not late to the party on this.

> But only he who sees, takes off his shoes;
> The rest sit round it, and pluck blackberries.[4]

I love that. "Only he who sees . . ."

Not everyone sees. We can't see much at all when we're hurried and worried. But if today is the focus, and we're not attempting to control what we can't, well . . . we can see that Earth is, indeed, crammed with heaven; every common bush afire with a God who is not at all worried.

FIFTEEN

Monster to Miracle

We have reasons to trust in God's character.

I've learned one great way to be more relaxed and to live at peace is to be quick with this particular phrase: "I don't know."

This is huge for me. I used to want to be Mr. Answer for Everything. I collect facts and figures in my head, out of some weird fear that someone will find me lacking for not knowing the capital of Albania, which is Tirana by the way. I just looked it up.

I know people have good questions about God, including many people who are deconstructing their faith. Why do things happen a certain way? Why does God allow this or that? Most of the time, I just plain don't know. I've learned it's good to say it out loud.

It's a very freeing thing, this not-knowing-and-admitting-it thing.

Being at peace doesn't mean knowing and understanding everything. That's a good thing, because we can't pull it off. It means simply trusting the character of God.

My friend Sy wrestled with God. He suffered throughout his life with deep emotional wounds from his childhood. He suffered physically, too, ultimately dying from cancer. But he told me that this is what faith is: having confidence in God's character and capability, knowing that one day your loyalty to God will be vindicated.

> This is what faith is: having confidence in God's character and capability, knowing that one day your loyalty to God will be vindicated.

"One day I will know the rest of the story that eludes me now," he said. "Therefore I deliberately choose to continue to be confident in God's character and capability—in spite of unjust circumstances and painful challenges that provoke me to question and doubt."

So yes, I have questions too. Big ones. But I keep seeing reasons to trust God. I keep seeing that style of His at work, how He operates. How difficult or tragic things happen, and there He is at the end of it, proving He was there all along.

I keep seeing how He makes things beautiful.

I wish you could meet my friend Ben. Maybe you will someday. I mostly like him because he's smart-funny and he makes me laugh.

I know him because of his work with CURE. Ben wasn't planning to start a hospital, but that's exactly what he wound up doing. And, wow, is it a special hospital, which I visited with Ben not long ago. It's in Mbale, Uganda. I loved hearing the backstory. It's really good.

Dr. Ben Warf is a neurosurgeon who wanted to be a missionary doctor, serving the poor somewhere in the world. A strange thing happened, though: Many Christian missionary-sending organizations wouldn't send him. They rejected his application.

The reason? Ben's daughter Sarah.

He and his wife, Cindy, have six children, but Sarah is special. She was born with elephantiasis, and her appearance is greatly disfigured. Ben says people continue to stare at her in shock. Sarah is now an adult who lives with Ben and Cindy.

The Christian organizations said they couldn't send Ben and family into the field because people would see Sarah and believe the family was cursed. People would not want to come close. They would recoil at the shame of Ben's family, and this would reflect badly on their mission.

But when Ben asked to work with CURE, he got a very different reception. After all, this is a hospital network that serves kids with disabilities and knows what they're up against.

Ben and his family of eight took off for Uganda to start a hospital.

And a weird, wonderful thing happened.

While people who saw Sarah did, in fact, presume she was cursed (in keeping with ideas about disability in many traditional cultures), they also saw something else, something they almost couldn't believe: not only did a respected American doctor and his wife also have a child with a disability, but . . . *they loved her.*

And they loved her completely. They were a family unashamed. They did not hide Sarah. They celebrated her. No matter what.

CURE-Uganda then began treating children with disabilities, kids also presumed to be cursed. They were the shame of their families. But the surgeon himself modeled God's love for them. As parents, they need feel no shame either. They could bring their little ones to the hospital and experience a completely different kind of love.

Rather than being disgusted that the Warfs would have such a child, they learned from them. And they learned to love Sarah too. Here's where it gets even better, if that's possible.

Ben and his family stayed for twelve years, and during that time Ben took note of the high incidence of hydrocephalus (water on the brain) among babies in the region. Hydrocephalus makes a baby's head swell, sometimes doubling or tripling in size. It's fatal if it's not treated.

In the US, it's dealt with quickly by installing a shunt, a way to drain the water from the brain. The problem: shunts fail. About half of them need to be replaced within a couple of years. And in Africa, Ben had a challenge: Most parents lived too far away from a hospital. Travel is too difficult. The child would be in dire trouble down the road.

So Ben developed a first-of-its-kind procedure, one that didn't require a shunt. It's revolutionary. It's now been used to save the lives of thousands of babies around the world. Ben's work has been featured in major newspapers and networks like CNN. He was given a MacArthur genius grant.

+

When a mom in Uganda notices her baby's head is swelling, it's a shock. She simply doesn't know what to do, or where to go.

Very often, she's not helped; she's judged. She's blamed. The community around her presumes she must have done something immoral, and that's why her child is a monster.

And "monster," by the way, is a thing people literally say. I remember the story of a little boy who developed hydrocephalus in a small village. His dad was the local butcher, and he and his wife had no idea what to do, or where to go, as the head continued to swell.

People marveled at the child and lined up to see him, freak show-style. People came from nearby villages to see "the monster."

The butcher and his wife heard about CURE, thankfully, and were able to get treatment at the hospital, the one Ben started. The swelling went down, and the child survived.

When people saw the baby boy afterward, they lined up again. People who had traveled to the village to see "the monster" were coming back to see him again and marvel for an entirely different reason.

They didn't call him "the monster" anymore. They called him "the miracle."

✦

People brought a blind man to Jesus and asked, "Whose fault is this?" "Who should be blamed?" "Someone obviously is immoral, and that's why he's cursed. But who is it? His parents? Or was it him?"

Jesus said something that must have shocked people. It still kind of shocks me, and I keep reading it: "'Neither this man nor his parents sinned,' said Jesus, 'but this happened so that the works of God might be displayed in him'" (John 9:3).

That's why. It's so we could see God in action.

Ben started a hospital in Uganda because of Sarah . . . and look what happened: thousands of "monster"-to-"miracle" stories.

Ben now teaches at Harvard while continuing the work in Uganda. He's trained more than thirty other neurosurgeons, mostly Africans, to perform the surgeries.

Sarah may never understand her role in all of this, of course. It's a lot for someone with mental challenges to take in. But what some say is a curse? It turns out to be a blessing.

This is how God operates, in little ways we don't see coming.

This is how God operates, in little ways we don't see coming. He turns curses around.

He turns curses around. He turns the world upside down.

This is what I'm in this for. There's so much of Christian culture I don't understand. I can't see the connection. But *this*?

Yes, I want to be part of this.

It's how God does things. I love how this is expressed in "Joy to the World." Now when I hear that song, and especially the third verse, I don't think of just Christmas. I think of little babies and thrilled moms and dads who feared they might be at a funeral soon, standing over a little box.

But funerals get canceled when Jesus shows up.

So do curses.

> *No more let sins and sorrows grow,*
> *Nor thorns infest the ground;*
> *He comes to make*
> *His blessings flow*
> *Far as the curse is found!*
> *Far as the curse is found!*

This is how the kingdom works. Do I have all the answers to every big question? No, I don't.

Have I learned to trust the character of God, through everything?

Yes, I have.

SIXTEEN

One Last Sunset

Peace we can't explain, and just in time.

A fair question: What about when there *is* a funeral? How do we have joy, this sense of well-being, in the event of possibilities that are almost too much to think about?

Of course, I'm not going to have any easy answers. But I once heard a story about a lawyer who lived in Chicago. Maybe you've heard it too. (I had to look it up to see if it was true, and it checks out.)[1]

The lawyer was very successful and admired by many. As a bonus, he also had an awesome lawyer-y name: Horatio Spafford.

He had a beautiful family too: his wife, Anna, and four little girls. They'd planned to travel to Europe by ship. A major business issue came up, so Horatio had to book himself on a later departure so he could stick around a few more days.

Anna and the girls went ahead. The French passenger ship they were on collided with a Scottish ship, and the result was devastatingly tragic. A sailor found Anna floating on a piece of wreckage. She survived, but all the girls were dead.

Anna sent a telegram to her husband: "Saved alone. What shall I do?"

Overwhelmed with grief, Horatio Spafford got on the next available ship to join his wife in Europe. During the voyage, he wrote some words that were eventually put to music. It became a hymn. I sang the song many times growing up in church, though I never could grasp the weight of it. It was originally named after the ship, the *Ville du Havre*, but eventually became "It Is Well with My Soul."

> *When peace like a river attendeth my way,*
> *When sorrows like sea billows roll,*
> *Whatever my lot, Thou hast taught me to say,*
> *It is well, it is well with my soul.*

It's a haunting story. I almost don't know what to make of it, because it's so hard to even think about a loss like that.

I can't imagine being in that state of mind. My kids are all gone? All of them? At once?

Honestly, I feel like I wouldn't be able to handle it, like it would be the very end of me. I don't think I'd have the resources to function at all, ever again, let alone write a poem about how my soul is somehow still at peace even in grief.

But I keep hearing stories like this from people. Not just stories from the 1800s, like this one, or other far-off "Amazing Heroes of the Faith"-type stories. I'm talking about people I personally know who've gone through tragedy. They'll say things like, "Somehow, I felt God around like never before," and "You know what? There was this peace I had somehow."

It doesn't make the pain disappear. Not at all. It accompanies the pain. The loss is real. The grief is real. The immense hurt is real. But so is this deep and persistent sense of well-being.

It seems there's a kind of peace that shows up only when you need it. Until then, you almost can't imagine having it. Maybe, like He does in so many other ways, God gives us what we need exactly when we need it, and not a moment before.

> Maybe, like He does in so many other ways, God gives us what we need exactly when we need it.

Paul wrote about this strange peace in his letter to the church at Philippi. It's "strange" because we can't really get our heads around it. It may make no logical sense to us. It just *is*. It "transcends all understanding," he said. And then he told us this peace is there to protect us. It will "guard" our hearts and minds (Philippians 4:7).

Jesus gave us a way of living that leads to peace, so He told us not to worry about tomorrow. We don't need to go there. That's not our business. There are enough problems in the world today to keep us occupied.

Might terribly sad things happen in the future? Of course. But that's not the end of the matter. Again, our hope is not naive. It's based on additional knowledge I can bring to mind: God is good, and death is not the last word.

And as for the future, I must trust that God will meet me there, in ways I can't now comprehend. I've seen Him do it for my friends.

One friend's wife passed away from cancer not long ago. She was a brilliant artist, and in her early forties. They had three kids. It hurts to think about. But my friend said a similar thing, that in his grief he experienced God in ways he hadn't before. He was devastated and bereft while simultaneously comforted. He struggled to explain it.

After she died, he posted a photo of a sunset, taken through a hospital window, with this caption: "Our last one together. Not bad. She thought so, too."

+

People will tell you that the key to ridding yourself of anxiety is to clear your mind. I find the opposite is true. Maybe I'm not doing it right. My mind just buzzes on. I can't seem to shut it down. I wind up getting aggravated at myself, which I'm pretty sure is not the objective.

I think it's interesting that Jesus' approach is the *opposite* of mind clearing. He told us to actively think about certain things. When He told us to consider the lilies, or think about the birds of the air, and how they're not worried, He was giving us something true to think about.

> **Jesus' approach is the *opposite* of mind clearing. He told us to actively think about certain things.**

Check out what Paul wrote about our mindset, right after the part about the peace that transcends understanding:

> Finally, brothers and sisters, whatever is true, whatever is noble, whatever is right, whatever is pure, whatever is lovely, whatever is admirable—if anything is excellent or praiseworthy—think about such things. Whatever you have learned or received or heard from me, or seen in me—put it into practice. And the God of peace will be with you. (Philippians 4:8–9)

If I want peace, I need to think about things—the right things, and not just positive-sounding things—and I have to start with what's actually true.

Instead of trying to think of nothing, I think about these sorts of things:

- I'm not in charge; the Lord is.
- He's very, very good.
- He doesn't hate me.
- He doesn't think I'm a loser.
- He knows me better than I know myself, and He loves me.
- I lack nothing; I have everything I need with Him as my Shepherd.
- There's a lot I can't control, and that's not a bad thing at all.
- I don't need to be afraid of a thing.
- He's got the big picture; I don't.
- God has continually been faithful to me during my entire life. He's earned my trust.

And if I don't trust Him, what's the alternative? I don't see many good ones around.

People put their trust in all kinds of people and things, and there are many worldviews to choose from. Most of them, however, don't make sense at a funeral.

People without God wind up playing "My Way" or "Over the Rainbow" or something. But Jesus stared death and suffering square in the eye and offers brilliant hope that there is still more to the story.

I don't know exactly what to make of suffering, of course. I do find the story of Job reassuring. It doesn't offer easy answers. But it gives us a God who simply rewards faithfulness. That's it. In the ensuing discussions with his friends, Job didn't have all the right answers. Not even close. He said some dumb stuff. But he wouldn't stop interacting with God.

Job's friends talked a lot *about* God. But Job talked *to* Him.

And in the end, God honored a humbled man who stayed faithful, despite Job's ignorance of the big picture behind his suffering.

Some people will say they don't believe in God because of suffering. They can't come up with a reason why He would allow that. I understand where they're coming from, but I also know that I don't know everything. Just because I can't come up with a reason doesn't mean a reason can't exist. My mind can't conjure up an exhaustive list of all possible reasons. When I'm humble, I'm quick to realize that.

When I watch surgeons do their thing in the OR, I don't often understand what's happening. I know that. When they ask for, say, a retractor, I don't think to myself, *I don't see the reason for a retractor here. Ergo, there is no reason.*

Why? Because I realize how very, very little I know.

So, like I say, I've learned to be quick with the "I don't know" response.

"Why did God allow that earthquake to devastate that poor village?"

I don't know.

"I prayed to get into that college. Why wasn't I accepted?"

I don't know.

Or like Jerry Seinfeld asked: Why *does* the pharmacist have to be two and a half feet up above everybody else?[2]

Yeah . . . I don't know.

I do know that the very Designer of us told us how we can have the joyful, peaceful life we are looking for, and He told us we shouldn't worry. He also told us to focus on this day, and even to pray for just this day's resources.

He told us to look at the animals. They're focused on today. When we're worried, consider them. Think about them.

> Just because I can't come up with a reason doesn't mean a reason can't exist.

As I type, our golden retriever, Cozy, is lying on the ground next to my feet. She's doing her goofy thing, lying on her back, paws in the air, basking in the sun in our little courtyard. I'm pretty sure that, like the lilies and the birds, she's not worried where her food is coming from tomorrow.

She's onto something.

Live author-n-dog
ACTION
SHOT

SEVENTEEN

Nigel, the Three-Legged Dog

Real love means we don't run from hurt, we feel it.

Real peace isn't about detachment, and real joy is deeper than mere happiness. (Remember the "regardless of circumstances" thing from earlier?) The only way we get to experience anything beautiful is by taking the risk of loving someone. Or something. Even something small.

Like a dog, for instance.

Getting a dog is a strange deal to make, if you think about it. Most deals don't work like this. It's hard to imagine a car dealer saying, "Look, buy this Hyundai and here's the best-case scenario: in about twelve years, you'll be bawling uncontrollably." C. S. Lewis wrote:

There is no safe investment. To love at all is to be vulnerable. Love anything, and your heart will certainly be wrung and possibly be broken. If you want to make sure of keeping it intact, you must give your heart to no one, not even to an animal. Wrap it carefully round with hobbies and little luxuries; avoid all entanglements; lock it up safe in the casket or coffin of your self-ishness. But in that casket—safe, dark, motionless, airless—it will change. It will not be broken; it will become unbreakable, impenetrable, irredeemable.[1]

Our dog Nigel died not long ago. He was fifteen.

I haven't been able to talk about it, not even with friends. I quickly change the subject. I can't handle the emotions. I'm serious. I'm going to try it now. Maybe in little bits and pieces.

I know this: God loves animals.

He created them, and He was very pleased. And what's more, when people try to discount or minimize just how important ani-mals are, I love to remind them that God's covenant with Abraham wasn't just with Abraham; it was with His animals too.

Think about that: God made a covenant with animals. They matter.

God sees when a sparrow falls. He notices one little bird.

If you're crying because your dog died, and anyone tries to tell you it's "just a dog," you tell them that thing about Abraham and the covenant.

There is no "just a dog."

Dogs are a big deal.

I got a note from my niece a few weeks ago. She's a young adult, embarrassed a bit by just how crushed she was by sorrow at the loss of her dog and how very much her dog meant to her. I told her some people just don't get it, and don't worry about what they think.

"They told me to get over it, and it's just a dog, and . . ."

No. Not "just a dog."

Grieve. It's okay. Don't listen to those people. And not just because *animals* matter, for dogs aren't mere animals. I love how

Matthew Scully put it in his marvelous book *Dominion*: dogs are God's "emissaries from the animal kingdom."[2]

Think about it: There are millions of animal species, and they're all scared of us. They run away in fear. Or, if they attack us, well, that's in fear too. They see us and head for the hills. It's all fright and fight and flight.

But dogs . . . ?

Dogs like us better than they like other dogs.

So many species, so much fear and alienation. But dogs come bounding, ears bouncing.

Here's one furry beast, something wholly other, that somehow crosses the divide from animal to man, and with a wagging tail. It wants to lick us on the face.

✦

Truth is, I didn't even want a dog at the time we got Nigel. We already had a dog, and she was a handful. But I'd scheduled a doggie adoption drive on my radio morning show and asked the shelter to bring in a "sample" dog we could talk about and pet while we were on the air.

They brought in the sorriest-looking beagle-mix-mutt-thing of all time. He was not only scraggly and downcast; he was missing fur on one side of his body.

Also missing: one leg.

They said he was a stray and they found him after he was hit by a car. They did surgery on him, but no one wanted to adopt him.

I called him to me. He ambled over and sat down and just leaned into me. That's it. He leaned against my leg the entire morning show. I had no chance. I had to call my wife. "Uh . . . there's this dog leaning against me, and he's missing a leg, and . . ."

Our doggie adoption radio drive totals for the morning? One whole (mostly whole?) dog was adopted. By the morning show host.

"Nigey" used to run with me. I'd go out jogging, and he loved it. Brant and Nigel, tethered, running miles together. At first I thought before long runs, *Wait, can he do this? He has only three legs* . . . And then I remembered I have only two.

Enough feeling sorry for him! Nigey had 50 percent more legs than I do.

He had a different gait, to be sure. Kind of a limp-gallop. I remember once when I sprained my ankle while we were running. I had to stop running and try to hop home. I remember passersby staring at us.

I guess the sight of a three-legged dog being walked by a one-legged-hopping guy was entertaining.

✦

Kids take it hard when they lose a pet. I think parents take it harder.

Because (and here's where the tears are inevitable for me) when we buried Nigel—and I know this isn't logical, but still—it felt like we were burying even more.

In my heart, his lifespan wasn't just fifteen human years. Those were some of the sweetest years of my life. They were years of our boy and girl growing up. We got Nigel when they were nestled in our home. We made up songs and stories about him. He was one of us.

Now they were out of the house on their own, and I was standing by a hole on a chilly, gray morning, and I felt like I was saying goodbye to even more than just a precious animal.

That's why parents feel it. It's all the memories. It's another kind of ending altogether.

Good grief. I just went through about fifteen tissues writing about it.

So will dogs be in heaven? Yes, of course they will. And no, I can't quote a Bible verse, but I'd bet the house on it. Heaven will be a restored earth. Things will be set right.

And an earth without dogs? Messed up.

There are certainly plenty of biblical references to animals in God's new creation. I've already mentioned God loves all that He made. When we told Nigel—as we did 43,902 times—that he was "a good boy!" we were so truly, deeply right. When God created animals, He said they were good. He beat us to it.

What's more—and you may think I'm being crazy—I suspect something else about heaven: I think we'll be able to clearly communicate with animals. I hope I'm right because I have many questions that need answers. ("So, Arfy, let's now discuss why, only when guests came over, you'd walk around our living room licking the floorboards, and . . .")

Yes, I have many reasons for thinking they'll be able to talk, but they mostly boil down to the fact that kids in every culture seem to imagine it and yearn for it.

You might think it's playful or silly.

Maybe. But again: I think our yearnings point us home.

Since living with real "joy" doesn't mean avoiding hurt, this peace is not about a zen-like detachment from pain. It's the opposite. It means feeling pain, owning it, and still trusting in the goodness of God.

The God of the Bible is anything but a God of detachment. The God of the Bible comes closer. He becomes one of us. He takes on our pain and heartbreak. He doesn't detach; He attaches.

He actively cares, and He cares deeply. He is "close to the broken-hearted" (Psalm 34:18), and when we are walking through the dark places in life, we're not there alone. He is with us.

If I'm going to be a friend like He is, I don't run away from my human friends and neighbors when they are suffering or mourning. I go toward them.

Truth is, dogs and humans, ocelots and oceans, stars and sparrows, all get their significance from their Creator, and His caring isn't in short supply. There's enough to go around.

So we care too. And while we can try to minimize pain (as in, "It's just a dog"), we're subtracting value from something beautiful.

That's not the way to peace.

> If I'm going to be a friend like He is, I don't run away from my human friends and neighbors when they are suffering or mourning. I go toward them.

If you've ever really loved, you know pain is part of the deal. Oh, how we can hurt. And I've learned I need to be more open to hurting. But for people who trust God's goodness, despair is fleeting. It's not the dominant musical note underscoring our lives. This mysterious sense of well-being? That's still somehow there.

Nigey was buried in "Nigey's blanket." We always put it in his bed so he'd be comfortable and he'd have something that smelled just right to him.

He was a very quiet dog. He didn't bark. He was a kindly, sweet, gentlemanly dog.

The last time I was with him, he leaned into my leg and let me pet him. That's all he really wanted. Just like the first time, you know?

He was an odd little dog. A misfit. But a very good emissary, indeed, to the misfit writing this sentence.

EIGHTEEN

0.000004409171076
Pounds of Awesome

God is at work in ways we can't fathom.

I've struggled to get my head around how God can know me and love *me*, specifically. And it's not just that I sense I'm unlovable—which I often do—it's because there are eight billion of us.

How can every single one of us be significant to God? We're each supposed to cast our cares on Him and trust that those concerns matter? All eight billion of us? That's a big number. Or maybe it's not, really?

It's relative, I guess. What's a big number to God? I can't get my head around it. For example, experts think you have about one hundred billion neurons in your brain right now.[1] Sure, maybe you feel that number dipping slightly as you read my writing, but anyway that's more than *ten times* the number of humans on the planet.

Or consider the stars. Experts think there are a *septillion* stars in the universe: I'm going to type what that looks like: 1,000,000,0 00,000,000,000,000,000.[2] (Yes, twenty-four zeros.)

If you do the math—and you won't, as you have better things to do even if I clearly don't—that means if we divided up the stars and gave them to people, each of us would get 125,000,000,000,000,000 stars. That's 125 quadrillion personal stars for me, and 125 quadrillion stars for you.

Now, I know what you're thinking: *Brant, please do some more math and tell us more about it. More and more. Never stop.*

Okay then, here you go: Say you were to then visit your stars and spend just one day on each of them (forgetting the travel time). It would take you more than 342 billion years to do it (not factoring in the extra days from 1,368,000,000 leap years).

Or think about the number of atoms in a single cell of your body: How many atoms are in your whole body? Somewhere around seven octillion.[3] That looks like 7,000,000,000,000,000,000,000, 000,000—give or take. So that's seven billion billion billion. Yep.

The point of doing this, besides the fact that it's cool, is to remind ourselves that maybe a loving Creator of the universe isn't overwhelmed, even if we are.

God transcends time. He's not in a hurry. He's not too busy for us after all.

Maybe eight billion humans aren't that many in God's economy? Maybe it's a very small number. We wonder how He could possibly have time to listen to us, but He's not subject to time. God transcends time. He's not in a hurry. He's not too busy for us after all.

You or I might see ourselves as insignificant, and our concerns as surely meaningless to our Creator. But we have our way of valuing things and people, and He has His.

Like when we see someone well-known, or some leader person, and we think, *Now this person is worthy of my time right now. This person is a VIP.*

Jesus? He puts VIPs on the back burner and opts to focus on NSWPs (No Status Whatsoever Persons). It happens in Luke 8, when a big-time synagogue leader begged Jesus to come to his house and heal his dying daughter.

There was a huge crowd around. The crowd was mentioned repeatedly (it "almost crushed him," it says in verse 42). And in that crowd was a woman who was socially rejected because of a bleeding issue. She was unclean.

She was not even supposed to be there. But she was desperate after years of suffering. She reached out and touched the hem of His garment, most likely the tassels on His prayer shawl.

Jesus stopped everything. Record scratch. Zoom in. Everyone else went to the blurry background. He focused entirely on her.[1]

Meantime, there was still the VIP synagogue leader, Jairus. He was put on the waiting list. The "unclean" woman was the top priority right then and there. Jesus didn't chastise her for breaking the cleanliness laws. No, He used a term of endearment and then healed her. "Daughter, your faith has healed you. Go in peace" (v. 48).

Then Jairus learned it was too late. They'd waited too long. Or so they thought.

While Jesus was still speaking, someone came from the house of Jairus, the synagogue leader. "Your daughter is dead," he said. "Don't bother the teacher anymore."

---

1. I love what Kyle Idleman said about this in his book *One at a Time* (Grand Rapids, MI: Baker Books, 2022). He called this the disappearing crowd because Jesus was fully present with this woman. The crowd wasn't even mentioned again. Honestly, how many modern Christian leaders would put a crowd on hold for someone with no connections or status?

Hearing this, Jesus said to Jairus, "Don't be afraid; just believe, and she will be healed."

When he arrived at the house of Jairus, he did not let anyone go in with him except Peter, John and James, and the child's father and mother. Meanwhile, all the people were wailing and mourning for her. "Stop wailing," Jesus said. "She is not dead but asleep."

They laughed at him, knowing that she was dead. But he took her by the hand and said, "My child, get up!" Her spirit returned, and at once she stood up. Then Jesus told them to give her something to eat. Her parents were astonished, but he ordered them not to tell anyone what had happened. (vv. 49–56)

Of course they were "astonished." I'm reading this two thousand years later, and *I'm* astonished by the entire story.

I mean, the important guy's daughter was *dying*. She was fading fast, while the no-status woman had been dealing with a bleeding issue for twelve years. Who in the world would look at the two of them and know that the bleeding woman was the priority right now? Jesus apparently did.

The Bible is full of these sorts of things: God weighing things differently than we ever would. To pick another of a hundred examples, imagine two Moseses: (1) a young, strong, motivated Moses with access to the royal family of one of the most powerful empires in the world, and (2) a broken-down, reluctant eighty-year-old Moses who'd been living off the grid in Nowheresville for forty years.

Which would you choose to lead slaves out of captivity? God waited for the old version and then said, "Okay, *now* I will use this guy. Now he's going to start doing some serious Moses stuff."

I think it's safe to say God enjoys working this way. I'm pretty sure He gets a kick out of it.

Jesus said the kingdom of God works like a mustard seed, which brings up more math fun, because guess how much one of those weighs? Two milligrams,[4] which is precisely 0.000004409171076 pounds. Or, for simplicity's sake, feel free to round that off to 0.0000044.

> You think something is insignificant? It's really nothing? Surprise! It's everything.

When a mustard seed is planted, Jesus said, "It grows and becomes the largest of all garden plants, with such big branches that the birds can perch in its shade" (Mark 4:32).

Smart, scholarly people have been discussing this little parable/analogy for centuries, teasing out all sorts of meanings from just a few words. There's a lot of depth here.

But at least one takeaway is this: the kingdom works in ways you don't see coming.

You think something is insignificant? It's really nothing?

Surprise! It's everything.

There was once a very sick boy named Michael. He was born in Sudan and spent years in a refugee camp in the middle of a civil war. At ten years old, he could barely move. No one had any idea what to do. No money, no access to medical care, no status. He was spindly. He couldn't walk. In fact, he was slowly dying, right there among the tents.

I know about him because a team from CURE's hospital in Kijabe, Kenya, found him. He wound up at the hospital in the care of CURE's lead surgeon there, Dr. Tim Mead, who realized Michael had a tuberculosis infection in the vertebrae of his upper back. It paralyzed the little boy and had even damaged his trachea.

Tim said that when they put a tube in his chest the first day

at the hospital, Michael stopped breathing and went into cardiac arrest. They had to operate immediately.

After the surgery, Michael's motor skills began to come back, and he was able to walk on crutches. But then he suffered a spinal cord stroke and was paralyzed again.

"He was so sick, we never thought he would live through this," Tim said. "Our spiritual team would come and pray over him every day. He learned to speak English, and we all became good friends."

Michael was paralyzed but alive. It was a very long, difficult recovery. He asked God, "Why did You do this to me?" and thought about going back to the refugee camp alone and in a wheelchair. He was heartbroken and depressed.

But this is when it gets better.

Tim's wife, Jana, served at the hospital and knew Michael. She said she heard Jesus telling her, *I want you to take care of him.* When she told her husband, Tim said, "Okay, if God said we have to take care of Michael, then we will take care of Michael."

So Tim and Jana went looking for schools. They found one willing to take him as a seventh grader. From his first day of school it was apparent: this was a smart kid. Michael excelled, ultimately winding up getting a college degree from Louisiana State University, where he was—get this!—named homecoming king.

I have the receipts because Michael Panther is a friend of mine, and so are Dr. Tim and Jana. The photos of Michael on graduation day in front of the LSU football stadium are priceless.

And it gets even better: Michael started a mission to help African kids like him, who need wheelchairs and other mobility devices. His organization is called Living With Hope (livingwithhope.net), and you should check it out.

Thousands of kids with disabilities now have mobility thanks to what God has done through Michael. I've seen photos of large gatherings of delighted kids getting their new chairs, and the joy is palpable. They can move about! They don't have to just lie there or wait to be picked up!

Honestly, who would have looked at ten-year-old Michael, sick and dying in a refugee camp, and thought: *Right there. That little boy. God will use him.* Nobody, right?

But the kingdom of God, you see, is like a mustard seed, and it grows and grows. And those little kids in the photos with Michael?

They're like precious, delighted little birds. Birds who now have a place to perch in the shade.

NINETEEN

Why the "Good News" Is Better Than You Think

The one King to rule them all.

Any "kingdom" that works like that? A kingdom where people like Michael get valued, honored, and elevated? Where teenage girls get to see their faces, for the first time, made whole? Where "monsters" are acknowledged as miracles?

Yeah, I'm not leaving that. I want more of that.

And if this kingdom is breaking through, that's some amazingly good news.

Of course, "good news" is what "gospel" really means. But "gospel" is another word that can really trip people up. Given my dysfunctional upbringing in church culture, it honestly used to make me inwardly cringe. I didn't understand what's so good about the good news. I associated it with church pews and sermonizing and wishing church would be over soon.

I knew it meant Jesus died for my sins, but that confused me when I read that He sent His followers out to share the gospel—before they even knew what the gospel was. I mean, Jesus hadn't died yet. His disciples didn't even know that was in the works regarding the kingdom and the good news that Jesus talked about all the time.

But I learned something not long ago: The word *gospel* actually predates Jesus. It had already meant something, and something very specific.

Kings come and go, and kingdoms do, too, of course. But when a new kingdom swept through a land in the ancient world, it wasn't uncommon to make an announcement to the vanquished. Messengers would be sent from the conquering king.

"Good news! The kingdom of [some guy's name] is here! You should be very happy! You're going to love it!"

There's an inscription on a stone that archaeologists found in Priene, Turkey, that uses the word *gospel*. It's an announcement about a king of peace. He's sent by God as a savior! No one can ever surpass him! His kingdom is good news—the gospel!

Here's the weird thing: It's not about Jesus at all. It's about Caesar Augustus. It's from 9 B.C.

Since Providence, which has ordered all things and is deeply interested in our life, has set in most perfect order by giving us Augustus, whom she filled with virtue that he might benefit humankind, sending him as a savior, both for us and for our descendants, that he might end war and arrange all things, and since he, Caesar, by his appearance (excelled even our anticipations), surpassing all previous benefactors, and not even leaving to posterity any hope of surpassing what he has done, and since the birthday of the god Augustus was the beginning of the *good tidings* [or "gospel"] for the world that came by reason of him.[1]

You can imagine being on the periphery of a powerful empire and one day everything changes. A new ruler takes over, bringing a new way of life. It might be Alexander the Great. It might be Rome. But they announce the gospel, the good news that now you're a part of their awesome kingdom! Better roads! Better schools! Better . . . whatever! You should be thankful to have such a king.

Most scholars think Rome was at its zenith under Caesar Augustus, that he was the most powerful Roman ruler ever. And to help rule their expansive kingdom, Rome had partnered with one of the richest men in history, one who couldn't be ignored: Herod the Great.

Herod wasn't just rich. He's one of the richest, most powerful people in world history. He controlled the all-important spice trade. He built fifteen massive palaces for himself. In one case, he wanted a palace atop a mountain, which presented an engineering challenge because . . . there wasn't a mountain there. So he did what most of us do: he forced thousands of people to build a mountain for him.

He put another massive palace on top of it, along with accoutrements like a personal 250-seat amphitheater and a giant swimming pool. Then, in a true alpha move, he named it Herodium after his awesome self.

Herod was about pure power. So was Rome. "The Eternal City" conquered the world with military might and brilliant hierarchical organization. Resistance was futile. Everyone would surely be assimilated.

And into this, at this exact historic moment . . . good news: God's kingdom invaded.

Perfect timing. The King Jesus arrived, and royal messengers were sent out to trumpet the news. Oddly, they skipped telling the important people and went straight to shepherds.

The King of kings was born when and where? Of all the possible places in the world, at all the possible times, Jesus was born in the reign of Caesar Augustus (the "savior" himself) and in Bethlehem, which sits directly next to—would you believe it?—Herodium.

Jesus was born in the very shadow of the greatest earthly power. It sure seems like God was making a statement: His kingdom is very, very, very different.

✦

The arrival of God's kingdom on earth wasn't announced in the halls of nobles, or even to workers on the day shift. It was announced to the night crew at the sheep farm. And baby Jesus wasn't placed in a gilded crib; He was wrapped up and put in a stone feeding trough, just as shepherds would do with spotless lambs to be sacrificed. This King wasn't here to enslave us; He would give Himself up for us.

Jesus grew up and then went up on a hillside to explain how this kingdom works: This kingdom is good news for the poor. Even those who mourn will be happy. His kingdom is good news for, of all people, the meek! How about that? Even the spiritually bankrupt will be happy!

Yes, this kingdom is . . . strange. What other kingdom would announce itself that way? Imagine Julius Caesar showing up in Gaul and saying, "I'm taking over and you know who's going to love it? *Meek people!*" No one does that.

But the people on the outs can celebrate. Because this is where what God wants done . . . gets done.

Jesus went about not just talking about the kingdom but *showing* people what it looks like: He healed the sick. People who couldn't even dare to hope to walk? They got up and walked. Lepers were made clean. The deaf could hear. The blind could see.

This was how Jesus demonstrated that the kingdom is among

us, and it's how He's still doing it through His people. This kingdom works like nothing else. It's way better. In what other kingdom can people like me get to come into the presence of the King, at any time of my choosing, and He actually listens to me? There's a place nearby called Tire Kingdom, and I can't even get through to the manager without being put on hold.

This kingdom is available to anyone, anyone at all, who wants it. There's no waiting. It's available right this second. It's not a matter of having a religious education or whether you have an impressive spiritual résumé. You don't even have to be a good person. You don't have to be smarter than average. Jesus said even kids get it. It's open to them and any of us humble enough to be like them.

> In what other kingdom can people like me get to come into the presence of the King, at any time of my choosing, and He actually listens to me?

If you don't see it already, I hope by the time you're done with this book you'll see that this kingdom is fantastic news, and such a revitalizing, energizing, even fun (!) alternative to the other kingdoms that demand our allegiance.

Here's another nice feature of the kingdom of God: it's permanent. You can put your all into it and never lose a thing. You simply don't need to worry.

No one even talks about Herod much, except when we talk about the baby born in his shadow. No one's celebrating his birthday by exchanging gifts and decorating trees and stuff. Probably.

My point is this: The kingdom of God will outlast them all. Every single power structure; every royal family; every government; every banking system; every mighty army; every seemingly insurmountable, immovable ruler . . . all will pass away. But this is the kingdom that simply can't be shaken, and that is the basis for this joy, this sense of well-being that transcends circumstances.

Herodium? That fortress is gone. The other King? That kingdom will endure forever.

Speaking in Music

Eternal life has already started.

When we see glimpses of God's kingdom, they're beautiful. But we live in an in-between, very awkward time. And as I typed that last sentence, I remembered one of my all-time favorite *The Far Side* comic panels.

The drawing is of a caveman trying to balance himself with a stick while a pterodactyl bonks his head flying into a tree. In the distance is a T. rex tripping over a rock. The caption is "Although it only lasted 2 million years, the Awkward Age was considered a hazardous time for most species."

I'm still laughing at that. Maybe you'd have to see it to fully appreciate it. I mean, I'd print it here but . . . lawyers.

So here we are, waiting for that new beginning that we trust will happen. When He "will wipe every tear from their eyes" (Revelation 21:4) and we get to see every sad thing come untrue.

> Blind eyes will be opened,
> deaf ears unstopped,
> Lame men and women will leap like deer,
> the voiceless break into song. (Isaiah 35:5 MSG)

I've gone to sports events. Nothing big like the Super Bowl, but some college basketball games and so forth. I went to an English Premier League soccer game recently, and the crowd energy was electrifying.

I can't imagine what it would be like to witness people who went from living their whole lives unable to see to having their eyes opened fully. Or to watch as crowds of people who have never walked *all* get up and walk and run and dance and "leap like deer" together.

As for the voiceless suddenly breaking into singing? I want to be there for that too. I heard someone say that music might be how we all communicate in heaven. That seemed odd to me, until I realized: Wait, we won't be speaking in English. Or Italian. Or Tagalog or Swahili or even—my personal preference—Elvish.

But music, the likes of which we've never heard? That translates. Maybe we'll be so freed from our limitations and our inhibitions that we'll just speak the most beautiful new music to each other, and we'll never, ever stop creating beauty. Sounds crazy, maybe, but you know what? I think it's a safe bet.

But again, for now, here we are. It's awkward because we're waiting for that.

The waiting isn't passive, though. There's plenty to do, plenty of incredibly joyful ways to be a part of the kingdom breaking through, little by little, into our daily existence. This is the fun part of life.

In biblical stories, it seems God was always looking for people to partner with, people who would walk with Him and let Him work in and through their lives.

You may not feel equipped to do this. If you feel incompetent, that's not so bad.

Honestly, I have a strong sense of "I don't think I can quite handle this" every morning before I do my radio show. How am I going to come up with things to say again? And how can I be entertaining? I sure don't feel entertaining.

So then I take our dog, Cozy, out for a walk. And during our walk, I talk to God out loud. I ask Him to please give me what I need for today, and what I need for today is creativity and energy and content. And I need a heart for people, the people who are listening to my words.

I've told Him I would love to see my influence expand. But only if it means my influence is really a way for His kingdom to grow on earth as it is in heaven.

Because I'm an introvert, I ask Him for social energy too. I know I will need it on an ongoing basis, but I ask for it just for today. I think that's what Jesus was telling us to do when He told us to pray that our Father would give us our daily bread. We ask Him for what we need just for today.

It puts me in a good place because I'm not thinking ahead to tomorrow's problems or potential disasters. Just today. That's it.

I walk by neighbors' houses, and I ask that His peace would be in each house. Doing that helps me love my neighbors, and I have more compassion for them. It turns my heart toward them. Instead of being annoyed by them, I'm rooting for them. All of them.

Cozy and I walk back home, and I sit down with a blank sheet of paper and try to come up with twenty things to say for the show. Each show seems insurmountable, and I think, day after day, *Okay, I somehow got yesterday's done, but now I'm starting over again?* But I've now done thousands of shows, and each time . . . it's there.

Whether or not I'm competent isn't the issue, is it? If God wants to partner with me, He can make stuff happen with what I can bring to the table, however simple or goofy I am. Same with you.

We humans can underrate the impact we can have. It's almost like we're scared of partnering with God, as Moses seemed to be at the burning bush. We think, *Yeah, well, of course God picked Moses, because he was a strong leader, but I'm just . . .* and so forth. But as we noted earlier, by this point Moses wasn't strong, and he sure wasn't leading anybody. He didn't want to lead anybody either.

> If God wants to partner with me, He can make stuff happen with what I can bring to the table, however simple or goofy I am. Same with you.

Most of us might have picked young Moses as leadership material. He was certainly bold and decisive and action oriented (and by "action oriented" I mean he killed a guy with his bare hands), but that wasn't when God picked him. Nope. God waited. When Moses got old and weak? *Bam*—now it's time.

God seems to prefer partnering with last-round draft choices. As a man who has always very much wanted to succeed at Guy Stuff but never quite could, I find this reassuring.[1]

---

1. True story: While I'm terrible with tools and have largely given up, I finally successfully did a "guy" thing and rented a tool from Home Depot. It was a pressure washer. And I did the pressure washing! I used it and didn't break it even a little bit, and I took it back on time. Very proud that I'd done a guy thing! I paid for the rental with my Visa and went home, feeling like a real man! The next day, the Visa people called. They reported "unusual activity" on my card and wondered if someone had stolen it.

In addition to lacking in some skill areas, I also happen to be a sinner, which means I often fail to properly love God and other people, all of whom are made in His image.

But I'm convinced God will work with anybody—anyone at all—and I'm not letting this sin thing stop me. I've decided I'm not going to do what I'm often tempted to do, which is either slink away in shame and just ignore God, or go the other way and try to justify how I've failed. Humans are very good at both of those things.

No, my plan is to keep partnering with Him. I'm going to keep showing up.

✦

I used to hear the story of Adam and Eve and take away the exact wrong lesson. I used to think, *See, they disobeyed, and now God is done with them.* But that's not what happened at all.

Adam and Eve disobeyed, but God didn't leave them. Ever.

He went looking for them. When they were hiding from Him, God said, "Adam, where are you?" which is kind of odd if you think about it. How would He not know where they were? But my understanding now is that God wasn't looking for GPS coordinates. The question "Where are you?" was more of a lament. Like, "What happened to you?"

What happened to our walks together?

Why aren't you showing up?

What happened to the thing we had going together?

It's honestly heartbreaking.

And I noticed something else too: Although Adam and Eve had to leave the garden, they didn't go alone. *God went with them.* He was still interacting with them, still involved in their family and lives.

They could still be with Him, still talk with Him, still partner with Him, and still trust Him. This is true for us too. While we're in this messy in-between time—waiting for the day when every tear is finally wiped from our eyes, and all that is wrong is made right and whole and perfect—eternal life with God has already begun.

I may be a sinner, but I'm not missing this opportunity. I don't want to ignore God and not show up. I don't want Him to ask, *Brant . . . what happened to us? Where are you?*

I'm not missing this. I'm showing up for my walk with God. And I'm bringing my dog.

A.I. simulation of Lawyers, if I used the "Far Side" thing.

TWENTY-ONE

Your Attention, Please

What you pay attention to determines the course of your entire life.

And here's the part of the book where I hit you with a riddle, which is weird because I haven't written it yet. In fact, I haven't written any riddles yet. This is my first attempt ever. I'm glad you were here for this.

We'll always have this moment.

Here we go. I'll describe something, and you tell me what it is:

- It's extremely valuable.
- Every person on earth has it to give.
- Millions of people are very interested in getting yours—rich people, poor people, people near you, and people you don't even know.
- I'm hoping I now have yours.
- And it's so valuable that even *God Himself* wants it from us. For real.

What is it?

I recognize this is probably not a good riddle. Riddle making is harder than I thought. I now suddenly have more respect for the Riddler from *Batman* because he must have been mentally exhausted all the time.

Anyway, the answer is . . . *attention*. Maybe I gave it away with the chapter title.

But yes, attention really is that big of a deal.

And while I hope to have yours, I'm honestly not even sure I can keep mine. As I'm typing this very second, sitting at a little table in the coffee area of a grocery store, I can't keep my eyes off this dog. Not my dog, but a mutt wearing a service-dog vest, and he's bounding around with great enthusiasm. He's also off leash. This must be violating some grocery store code, but he's irresistible.

Yes, I've got a book deadline, but how do you not watch that? You *have* to watch that.

He now has my attention. He earned it, with charm and his waggly ways.

And attention is a big, big deal.[1]

True story: When I started out in radio, I was a News Man. I capitalize this because I took it very seriously. It was a small station, and when they hired me as their first News Man, they moved me into an equipment closet, where I set up my News Command Center. (I called it that and made a sign.)

This was during a time of my life we call the Toast Phase, when

---

1. I kid you not. A lady just brought in *another* dog, and it is *on*. They are full-on barking and lunging at each other. In the store. While I'm writing. These sentence fragments. If you're looking to test your powers of concentration, try writing during a War of the Grocery Dogs.

I ate an entire loaf of dry, burnt toast every morning. That was my food plan. I realize this might sound odd to you, but it made sense to me at the time.

Anyway, to the News Command Center I brought a new four-slice toaster, a Proctor Silex with dual controls that could burn the toast just how I liked. I'd plug it in and toast away all morning while I worked at my computer, writing my newscasts that I would deliver every hour.

One morning, everyone started running.

I didn't know why. I was busy reading and typing and munching on my toast. There was a ruckus outside the News Command Center, mainly the general manager and the program director frantically running to and fro. They eventually descended on my NCC, looked at me, then at my toaster, then down at an outlet where I'd plugged it in, then back at me. Then they lunged to the outlet.

They unplugged my News Command Center Toaster and plugged another plug back in, one that apparently was connected to some kind of satellite-uplink thing deal. I think they said I had knocked the station off the air for thirty-two minutes.

Anyway, I should have paid attention to what I was unplugging, but I was excited about the toast. (In case you're wondering, I would totally still eat a loaf a day if I could. It's still delicious to me. I had to stop because I ran into some issues, and a doctor said I should try a special "balanced diet." It's not as delicious to me, but here I am now.)

I tell you that story because, hey, who among us hasn't done something like that? I'm sure it's not just me. Raise your hand if you haven't unplugged an entire media outlet to make something crunchy. That's what I figured: nobody.

I also tell you that story because attention is a thing we should think about more. Seriously: it's everything. Attention is the currency of our lives, the thing that matters most.

We "pay" attention, like we pay to attend an event. Our attention is limited, after all, so we have to figure out where it's going.

Sometimes it's a matter of life and death.

We see it very obviously in the stats about thousands of people who die each year from distracted driving in the US alone. Someone wants my attention for a second with a text? I can look at it and . . . accidentally end someone's life.

> Attention is the currency of our lives, the thing that matters most.

I've learned if I want joy in life, I have to pay attention to the right things. After all, we are all being formed, and the things that shape us are precisely the things we are paying attention to. That's why marketers buy lists with your name and contact info on them: they want a chance to get you to pay attention to them, even just a little bit, knowing that's the key to changing how you live. That's why advertisers buy billboards.

Can we make you think about flooring for a moment?

Or perhaps you need an injury lawyer named Bob?

Hey, how do you feel about this photo of some bacon?

Pay attention to this bacon, thank you, and now think about the Cracker Barrel that's just eight miles up the road.

As a kid, I wouldn't think about Kool-Aid that much. But I did become aware there was a giant living pitcher of Kool-Aid that apparently wanted my attention *really* bad. He was willing to do whatever it took. Chaos? Destruction? Not an issue. He would not let a brick wall come between him and our attention. We *will* be conscious of him, and we *will* then fully understand how to quench our thirst after a hot day of rollerblading. Attention *will* be paid. Oh yeah.

Marketers simply *must* have our attention. It's that valuable.

Imagine the shaping power of hundreds or thousands of hours of our attention dedicated to foolish things. Imagine the shaping power of scrolling online through anger-and-anxiety land for hours a day, while spending only a few moments a week talking with God or being reminded through Scripture of His goodness.

Of course we're going to wind up angry, and of course we're going to be fearful and anxious. What we pay attention to molds us completely. It's everything. I know I already wrote "It's everything," but seriously, it's everything.

People don't talk about this enough. We're such forgetful people too. God acknowledged this repeatedly in the book of Deuteronomy, when He was telling His people something like, "Look, you're going to get distracted, so you've got to build reminders into your life of our relationship. We belong to each other" (see 6:8–9).

So why does God *need* our attention?

Good question. And here's a good answer: He doesn't.

God doesn't *need* anything. He is completely without need.

But He knows this is how we will thrive. He wants us to experience His joy, which is our strength (Nehemiah 8:10). God wants us to go through life with a deep sense of peace. He knows if we forget about Him, we won't have it. It's that simple.

Every single thing we think about changes us. Perhaps in a beautiful way. Or in an ugly, distorted, damaging way. Leo Tolstoy, in his *A Calendar for Wisdom*, quoted Lucy Mallory: "Every thought a person dwells upon, whether he expresses it or not, either damages or improves his life."[1]

Maybe you're familiar with this verse: "We demolish arguments and every pretension that sets itself up against the knowledge of God, and we take captive every thought to make it obedient to Christ" (2 Corinthians 10:5).

> God wants us to go through life with a deep sense of peace. He knows if we forget about Him, we won't have it.

We really have to do that, the thought-capturing thing. Thoughts seem to just "happen," sure, but we can grab them, hold them up to the light of day, take a good look at them, and dismiss them if needed. We can say to ourselves, "Now that's a dumb thing to think about," or "That may not even be true," or "I need to move on from this and think about something else."

This isn't a guilt trip. It's an exciting opportunity. If we want God's joy in our lives, we need to pay attention. One of the most earnest and hopeful little books about this is a classic titled *The Practice of the Presence of God*, written in the seventeenth century by a French devotee known as Brother Lawrence:

> He does not require a lot from us—just a little remembrance of Him once in a while, a little worship, and sometimes to pray for His grace. Offer your troubles to Him and give thanks to Him for the blessings He has given you and continues to give you. In the midst of your troubles, comfort yourself with Him as often as you can. Lift up your heart to Him, even during meals and when you are in the company of others. The littlest remembrance will always be acceptable to Him.[2]

The slightest turn, a little nod, acknowledgment of His goodness in your life. Right in the middle of everything else. It matters so much.

Now that I think of it, I think this is how love works. I know my wife likes it if we're in a crowded party and I look over at her. I need to remember to do that more. Or maybe when she grabs my hand as people are demanding my attention, I willingly hold hers. There's a glint of recognition about to whom we belong.

It seems so small, but like I said . . . it's everything.

TWENTY-TWO

Is God on an Ego Trip?

How praising God is a source of peace.

Here's a fair question, and it's one I wondered about even as a kid: Why is the Bible so full of stuff telling us to "praise the Lord"? Isn't this kind of egocentric? Like this, for instance: "Praise the LORD, all nations! Extol him, all peoples! For great is his steadfast love toward us, and the faithfulness of the LORD endures forever. Praise the LORD!" (Psalm 117:1–2 ESV).[1]

Yes, He's great. His love is great. His faithfulness is great. I believe that. But I'm sure I'm not the only one to ask this question: If there's a real God who loves us and created those septillion stars we were talking about earlier, why on His green earth would He want us to bang on about how awesome He is?

---

1. By the way, I picked this little section to highlight because I have it memorized. Why do I have it memorized? I wanted to memorize a whole chapter of the Bible, and this is the shortest chapter of the Bible. It's just two verses. I feel pretty good about myself.

He already has everything. He already knows He's great, right? But He wants us to sing about Him over and over? Did He seriously create a race of beings because He wanted to hear about Himself?

To arrive at an answer, of course, it's helpful to remind ourselves that God is good. That's why He does anything He does.

> We are to speak about His good qualities because it reminds us of His good qualities. We need to do it because it helps us settle down and be less anxious.

No, He doesn't *need* us to praise Him. Not at all. As we mentioned in just the last chapter, He needs nothing. He tells us to praise Him because it's for our own good, and He loves us. Once again, He's showing us how to live a life of joy and peace in the middle of the world's chaos.

Singing songs about the goodness of God is very, very good for us. It takes our attention off lesser things and puts it on the most important things. We are to speak about His good qualities because it reminds us of His good qualities. We need to do it because it helps us settle down and be less anxious.

Let's go back to Philippians 4. It's wild to think this is how Paul wrapped up his letter, especially given that he was writing from prison:

> Rejoice in the Lord always. I will say it again: Rejoice! Let your gentleness be evident to all. The Lord is near. Do not be anxious about anything, but in every situation, by prayer and petition, with thanksgiving, present your requests to God. And the peace of God, which transcends all understanding, will guard your hearts and your minds in Christ Jesus. (vv. 4–7)

He was telling them to deal with their anxieties by being thankful and by talking to God about it. That's the route to peace,

he said. The whole letter is about joy, in fact. He drove home the point that it's not based on circumstances, and given that he was writing from prison, it's even more believable.

> But I will rejoice even if I lose my life, pouring it out like a liquid offering to God, just like your faithful service is an offering to God. And I want all of you to share that joy. Yes, you should rejoice, and I will share your joy. (2:17–18 NLT)

Please reread that, especially if you've been around church culture for a while, and Scriptures start to become like wallpaper to you. This guy was in captivity, and he was saying he was thankful for it, and that if he wound up losing his life, well, by golly, he'd enjoy that too.

The world is a madhouse. It's true. And yet . . . peace is right there on the table if we want it.

The people he was writing to had plenty of legitimate worries, by the way. They were in a fancy, cosmopolitan city, but in a larger culture that was very hostile to the ways of Jesus and His followers. Besides their own daily worries about family and health and finances, they were facing serious consequences for their faith.

But Paul told them to be thankful. Talk to God about what you're thankful for. Talk to Him about what you are anxious about. Rejoice, always. This is not papering over real worries; it's actually a way to wrestle them to the ground.

The world is a madhouse. It's true. And yet . . . peace is right there on the table if we want it.

I just took a break and (tactical error, here) checked social media. The first post I saw was from someone I don't even follow: "My blood is boiling!" with a news video. I didn't watch the video. I don't really want my blood to boil just now.

But I *could* click on it, I guess. It might give me a little dopamine satisfaction, somehow. Especially if it's about people whom I don't agree with doing that stuff they always do. I'll feel affirmed, which gives me a virtue hit, and I'll also feel informed, which gives me another virtue hit.

Or—horrors—maybe the video is about people like me doing stuff we do, and the poster's blood is boiling because of people like me, who are the good people. That would be horrible. I would need to reply. And that would mean fielding replies to my reply and thinking about those replies. But I would have defended the truth, which can make me feel good about myself.

So there's a lot going on there. A mix of feeling good about myself for being right and a good person, and perhaps nervousness about how people are responding to me while I try to do other stuff, like write this book. All while my blood is boiling. It's a big mix of a whole lot of motives and feelings and stuff.

What's not in the mix: *peace*.

This is because it's all about me. If I turn my attention, for just a moment, to saying true things about God, things change. I remind myself that I can trust Him and that He can't be shaken.

Peace is not far away.

+

When I was a kid, I had several small paperback books full of *Peanuts* comic strips. I read them and reread them.

To this day, I instinctively respond to negative stimuli by saying one of two things: Either "rats" or "good grief." It's interwoven into my personality.[2]

It shaped me. What we read and watch and think about? That's who we're becoming.

As we discussed in the last chapter: if I'm to be joyful and have this sense of well-being, regardless of circumstances, I have to put my mind on the right things. It simply won't happen otherwise.

So often, the writers of Scripture told us the "right things" are the things we're thankful for. It's not just Paul saying that this is the key to peace. It's a constant theme. Again, God doesn't *need* our thanks. He wants us to do it so we can live with joy.

It's a very practical thing, this gratitude. It chases out things that will destroy us. As I wrote in *Unoffendable*: "*That's the thing about gratitude and anger: they can't coexist.* It's one or the other. One drains the very life from you. The other fills your life with wonder. Choose wisely."[1]

There are people who will tell you not to be grateful. They'll tell you that this or that tragedy or this or that crime or this or that societal injustice means you shouldn't be thankful.

These are people deeply loved by God. These are also, sadly, miserable people.

They may be right about the wrongs they are perceiving. But once again, they have only part of the story. They are "informed," perhaps. Just not enough. They're awakened to the brokenness of the world, but they're still asleep, oblivious to the goodness of God that surrounds them daily.

God's goodness is the deepest reality. He's not just the author of life; He's the sustainer. He holds everything together. Everything that is beautiful is God's handiwork, even His beloved critics.

---

2.   I still think someone should develop a personality-typing system based on *Peanuts* characters. Forget the Enneagram or the Myers-Briggs. Are you a Lucy? A Charlie Brown? A Sally? I know for a fact I'm a Linus. I've always known this.

People can hate God, even try to ignore Him, and He lets them do it. And yet here they remain: walking, talking, living, breathing evidence of His true artistry.

"For we are God's handiwork," Paul wrote, "created in Christ Jesus to do good works, which God prepared in advance for us to do" (Ephesians 2:10).

But our translation "handiwork" doesn't quite catch it. Paul used a word that is rare in the Bible: the Greek word *poeima*, which means "poem."

> Not all of us are poets. But we're all poems. We are works of art, all of us.

Not all of us are poets. But we're all poems.

We are works of art, all of us, living amid an unspeakable beauty that begs us to try to speak it. I admire writers who have the descriptive power to take up the dare. When I'm not asleep to the whole story—when I'm not caught up in my own much smaller, deadening stories—I at least have the words "Thank you."

I heard a tip the other day about how to be grateful, and I want to pass it on.

Most of the time, we're left-brained about being thankful. We'll think, *Okay, what am I thankful for?* and we make a list. Maybe we write it down; maybe we just say things out loud or try to think of some things.

There's nothing wrong with that, of course. I'm one of those analytical, logical people who prefer to think about things at arm's length. I try to be dispassionate. I picture myself as Data from *Star Trek*. (Wait, wasn't I just Linus? I'm kind of a mash-up: Linus, Data, and you can also throw Gonzo from *The Muppets* in there.)

But here's the idea: bring the creative right brain into it.

Keep a running list, maybe on your phone, adding to it as you remember, of moments you are thankful for. Snapshots in life when you were very, very happy. Or in awe of nature. An experience you are so grateful you had. Maybe when you felt close to God or felt most secure. Maybe it's a person you are so glad you met, and it was the first time you met them.

I like to think about moments with people when we were both laughing *hard*. Not about something merely hilarious but, like, epic, continued laughter and riffing on the funny thing until we had driven it into the ground, and then we started it back up again and laughed hard again. That kind of thing.

Of course, then there's "That's the first time I held Julia" or "Justice kept giggling when we were playing one-on-one Wiffle ball in the front yard," and now I'm tearing up. That's okay. I think if Data had kids, we'd see his white makeup run.

But do it. Keep a list, and go back when you have thirty seconds to focus on one of the memories, one of the snapshots. Just camp out there for a bit. Say it softly if you like, but speak it out loud.

"Thank you."

TWENTY-THREE

The Investment Plan
You Can Color With

The direct connection between generosity and peace.

I'm no doctor, like Dr. Tim or Dr. Moyo or the other surgeons I've gotten to know. I can't even win at Operation, the game where the guy's nose lights up when your hand jiggles.[1]

But since I've gotten to visit a lot of these hospitals and observed many surgeries, I'm so pleased to tell you that the real doctors are remarkably caring and competent, and that at no point in the surgeries does anyone's nose light up, neither patient, nor surgeon. Nobody. There are also no buzzers.

I may not be a medical professional, but one thing I *can* do very well in the CURE hospitals is color things with crayons. I

---

1.   A quick aside, from a non-medical professional: Anyone else alarmed that his eyes are
      wide open the whole time we're operating on him?

try to stay humble about this, but I may be the best there is at this "procedure." I sit in the ward with the moms and the little patients and color with them. Once again, I don't mess around. I color with verve and style. I color with panache, a certain *je ne sais quoi* and a *joie de vivre* . . . and I actually failed your French class but look at me now, Madame Edwards. *Inarrêtable.*

Anyway, even though I don't have the best social skills, I can sit comfortably with people for hours if some crayons are involved.

These are kids who, again, because of their disabilities, aren't just in poverty. They're often rejected by everyone but their own moms. Even the slightest disability is considered a curse in many cultures, and people will not only mock the child but they'll also ostracize the family from the community entirely. No one wants a curse to spread. The mom is often abandoned by her own husband if she chooses not to turn her back on their cursed little girl or boy.

I get to play with kids who aren't used to having anyone play with them at all. And I'd bet you would enjoy it too.

So this is easy duty, finding people to color with me. Oftentimes I'm coloring not just with six-year-old girls but with seventeen-year-old guys, who are just as delighted to be included.

Once, I brought a small blue rubber ball into the children's ward. It was fun, but it kind of hurts to think about. A teenage guy in his bed enthusiastically bounced it back and forth with me for over an hour until I had to leave. When you're not used to any interaction at all, well . . . I guess it's an experience you don't want to end.

And now I'm thinking about Adem. He's a teenager in Kenya. When he came to CURE, he asked the lady who brought him, "Why are they talking to me? Why are they smiling at me?"

This is because it was all very strange to him. The bright colors, the busy atmosphere, and the fact that people treated him like a human.

Adem wasn't called "Adem" by his own family. They called him "the Baboon" because he couldn't stand upright. He was born with a condition that forced him to move about on all fours. He did it remarkably well, all things considered. He lived in a remote hillside village and worked as a shepherd.

This shepherd moved about on hands and feet, among the sheep, talking to them and flicking little pebbles at them to move them this way or that.

When Adem was told he would be taken to a hospital that might be able to heal him, he was in disbelief. But that's exactly what's happened. He can now stand up straight and walk. I remember knowing his story and then seeing video of his first steps on the therapy bars, smiling from ear to ear.

Adem was told about a God who heals, a God who loves him. A God who knows who he is. He's not "the Baboon."

He's Adem.

✦

Oh yes: I was going to write this chapter about the close relationship between joy—this deep sense of well-being—and giving.

It says on American money, "In God We Trust," and I know some people protest that, and others protest the protest. I'm not sure it's a true statement for our culture, but I do like the reminder of how I should live—In God I Should Trust—so I hope we keep it.

I do wonder if I've really trusted God with my money. I honestly suspect many people who say they want to follow Jesus don't really trust Him with their money. (Or maybe they don't trust the people who are collecting the money in Jesus' name. I certainly understand that.)

But there's a verse from Proverbs that I'll occasionally read on the air, and it usually gets the reaction, "That's seriously in the Bible?"

If you help the poor, you are lending to the LORD—and he will repay you! (19:17 NLT)

It really says that. Even the exclamation point! I didn't add that.

So if my resources go to the poor, to people who can't do anything for me, God will cover it. He always does. He *will* repay me, it says.

I occasionally get from listeners, "Yeah, but you can't really 'lend' anything to God," and they get theological about it. But I keep reading the verse, and you know what? It keeps on saying the thing it says.

I don't know what to do with that, theologically. I just know it says that, so I'm going with it. I am but a simple man.

Lending to the Lord is an interesting idea. Will I *really* be repaid?

What's God's credit rating? Is it 650 or higher? Can I really trust this deal? Can I have "In God We Trust" belief for real?

Our banking system—our entire economy!—is based on just that: trust. The root word for "credit" is the same as "credibility." It literally means "trust."

People struggle with finding a trustworthy place for their money, one with a solid return. So maybe I trust a banker I've never met, or a broker I'll never see, or maybe a big corporation that will eventually vanish like a vapor.

Since God says that when we give to the poor we're actually lending to Him—and He *will* repay us—that seems like a really safe place to me. My guess is He's even a better bet than the FDIC, bonds, or a mutual fund.

It hasn't always seemed that way to me. I'm naturally selfish, and giving is something I'm growing into. I'm late to the party.

And that's just it—since it really *is* a party, I love how the BibleProject guys put it: "We're called to keep the party going."[1]

Growing up in church, I saw giving as a law. It drained the life out of it. There's a lot of context to the Old Testament idea of tithing that I wasn't told about, and here's part of it: In Deuteronomy, God told His people to set aside a tenth of all of their produce . . . for a giant party in His presence. Grain, wine, olive oil, cattle, sheep, wine or "other fermented drink"—all for a big joyous celebration (14:22–26).

And then every three years, it was supposed to go like this:

> At the end of every three years, bring all the tithes of that year's produce and store it in your towns, so that the Levites (who have no allotment or inheritance of their own) and the foreigners, the fatherless and the widows who live in your towns may come and eat and be satisfied, and so that the LORD your God may bless you in all the work of your hands. (vv. 28–29)

Now that sounds like a fun way to tithe. Who knew? And somehow, we've made this party into a solemn passing of a plate. Once again, God is more fun than we are.

God is always concerned about "the foreigners, the fatherless and the widows," and He's looking for like-minded people to partner with.

If you're reading this and feeling guilty, please stop it. Thank you. This isn't a guilt thing. It's another beautiful opportunity to step into community with God and bring His kingdom to earth as it is in heaven.

I've learned it's fun to conspire with Him, and with His people, to find ways to keep this party going. What I've also learned, as a naturally miserly person who's really enjoying this giving thing now: it changes my heart.

God is at it again, telling us something not just because it benefits others but for our own good. Giving is another ticket to

> It's fun to conspire with Him, and with His people, to find ways to keep this party going.

freedom from anxiety, because it's teaching me that God will always keep providing. He lacks nothing, and like Psalm 23 says, "I lack nothing" too.

That reinforces the daily sense that I'm secure, regardless of what happens. I can trust God's generosity. There is enough. Again: joy. I'm becoming a different person.

More secure. More patient. More content. I'm more fun at parties. Invite me. (I don't have to bring my accordion if you don't want, but I highly recommend . . .)

Giving is fun. It's not supposed to be done out of guilt. We're not supposed to burden people with it. It's a pleasure. We give, and we see again that God's faithfulness isn't a cliché. It's real.

You can take it to the bank.

Or don't. Take it to kids like Adem and the ones I get to color alongside, or be creative in your own world to keep the party going. God will repay you.

When? How? I have no idea. But He promises it. My own experience has been that the more we give away (specifically to the poor and marginalized and sick), the more we get back. But God is not a math formula or an ATM, and this isn't the prosperity gospel. This is simply trusting a God who says, *When you do it for one of these, you've done it to Me. And I've got you covered.*

Whoever paid for Adem's surgery? That was a very good investment. I think you'll be pleased at the returns if you're not already.

When it comes to investing, there's nothing wrong with mutual funds and cryptocurrencies (maybe), but they're not the only game in town. And if we're truly thinking long-term, they're not the best game in town either.

God, being not just loving but *fun loving*, gives us an investment option we can color with.

An investment plan that actually giggles. Who saw that coming?

TWENTY-FOUR

That One Time I
Killed That Thing

The joy of losing control.

One time, a real nice lady gave me a real nice plant for my office . . . and I done killed it. It was tall and lush and green and full and beautiful, and I gave it the ol' *Extreme Makeover, Neglect Edition,* and turned it into a crusty brown pile of detritus in a pot.

I didn't know where to throw it out. So after I killed the plant, I put the pot formerly known as "plant" out on the veranda, which is a commons area for all the organizations in our building. That way, no one would know who abandoned the pot-o'-nothing. I'm a class act.

The radio studio shares a wall with the veranda. I looked out the window during the show one morning and noticed this prim, bookish, middle-aged lady—someone I still haven't met—watering the dead plant. Naive but, you know, sweet. But mostly naive.

She came out and did this every single day. I'd be on the air, notice some movement to my right, out the window, and there she was, watering and trimming the dead plant.

And then the dead plant, which Brant Hansen killed, started growing. The dang thing started shooting up green. It grew and grew, and she kept trimming it, too, here and there. She kept watering.

One morning, I looked out and marveled: That plant that I, Brant Hansen, personally killed, was now more beautiful than when I had it in my office. It was back, better than ever. Glowing healthy! And it occurred to me . . .

I could take my plant back now.

It would look great in my office! I'll just go snag it sometime when no one's out there and bring it back in—you know, liven up the office for the me-meister!

I mentioned this to my wife, Carolyn. She said it wouldn't be right to take the plant back. She said it wasn't mine anymore.

She said that lady redeemed it, so it's hers now.

Amazing what love does.

✦

I think we all, deep down, no matter our religious views, sense that life is a gift. Like it didn't *have* to happen, but here we are, and we've been given a shot at it, so we need to justify getting this gift somehow. We need to prove ourselves, that we're good people and we deserved this.

I think it drives us, in fact. Watch people who seem to have everything—like a celebrity: a mansion in LA, great looks, a lifetime to travel the world—and they'll spend a lot of time telling us what they're trying to do to be a good person. They feel like they must justify what they have. It's very human.

But if you ever start to think you're not really a good person (a very rare thought, since something like 85 percent of us believe we are morally better than the average person[1]), you might then be freed up to admit that maybe someone else should be running this show.

We've all been given a kingdom, a sphere of control. But what if it's like when Fulin became emperor of China? He needed help. He was five. Or Edward, who became king of England when he was nine? Other people had to run their kingdoms for them. They didn't know what they were doing.

(I'm building up to a powerful point here, but I can't help but think if I took over as king of America at age nine, things would actually have been pretty awesome. My cabinet? From *The Muppets*: Sam the Eagle is secretary of defense. Animal is secretary of energy. Rowlf is obviously surgeon general. I can do this all day.)

Maybe you had this nightmare as a kid—I've heard it's common: Your mom leaves you in a car by yourself for a bit. Then the car starts rolling down a huge hill in a city. You have to take over . . . but you don't know how, and your feet don't reach the brakes. I trusted Mom to drive the car. I did not trust me, and for good reason.

> Who *do* I trust to run this life I've been given? Am I really the best choice?

It's an honest question: Who *do* I trust to run this life I've been given? Am I really the best choice? Should I go with my instincts and desires, or should I look elsewhere? And if I do look elsewhere, who is best for this job?

There's a famous passage in Proverbs that says:

> Trust in the LORD with all your heart
> and lean not on your own understanding;
> in all your ways submit to him,
> and he will make your paths straight. (3:5–6)

I've always really wondered: *Okay, but in real life, what does this look like?*

I'm still learning. But I do know now that so much peace is found in simply doing the things Jesus told us to do. Again, because He's truly good, the things He's telling us to do help us thrive. He's like the lady with my former plant. He *knows* how to make us flourish. His way is the way that brings a sense of well-being, no matter what is happening around us.

Jesus told His disciples at the Last Supper that He was leaving them with a gift; it was something no one else could give, and it would be the best gift ever. He even said it's a gift the world doesn't give: "Peace I leave with you; my peace I give you" (John 14:27).

A few verses earlier, He said that He would give it to those who obey Him. He is the Way that leads to a quality of life that we are made for. It's a life we can have now.

I have decided to accept this gift. It's a very, very good gift. I do not want to return this gift. I mean, what would I rather have than peace? What would anyone want more?

Weirdly: we choose other stuff all the time. All of us do. It's like Jesus is giving us the thing He knows we really want, and we know (if we think about it at all) that we really want it, but just after we say, "Thank you!" we're looking for the receipt so we can take it right back to Kohl's or something.

And how many times do we exchange our peace for the chance to read the latest news headlines and then everyone's commentary on said news stories? Many of us would apparently rather have that than peace. We'd rather doomscroll through social media than have peace. We'd rather nurse our anger than have peace. We're trading in the gift of a lifetime for . . . that? We should at least get some Kohl's Cash.[1]

---

1. One burning theological question: Do we have to tithe our Kohl's Cash?

It's dumb, but this really is how we operate. We pay attention to all the wrong things, then wonder where the peace and joy in life went.

> **We pay attention to all the wrong things, then wonder where the peace and joy in life went.**

God is showing us how to live through Jesus. It's a wonderful thing. I mean, words on a scroll or page can be wonderful, but there's nothing like a person to learn from. Jesus is the Word of God, made flesh. He is God's opinion.

When people first hear the idea behind my book *Unoffendable*, about anger and forgiveness, they think I'm nuts. In it, I make the argument that we're supposed to get rid of all anger and do it as soon as possible. I do this because God has forgiven me, and I'm to forgive others in the same way. I can't simultaneously forgive and hold on to my "right" to anger.

What does this *not* mean? That what they did is fine, or that I must stay in relationship with them.

What *does* this mean? Taking Jesus seriously and obeying Him.

When people first seriously consider living life *unoffended*, they say something like, "Wait, my anger isn't righteous anger?" But when I make the case, and people apply this teaching of Jesus to their lives, they find great freedom.

They change their expectations of the world, and they're daily humbled with the understanding of how much God has done for them. They learn not to try to control other people. They start seeing people through more compassionate eyes, as God sees them. They don't lie awake at night roiling with anger. Their relationships improve.

They have a more joyful life.

This is the kind of life hack Jesus keeps giving us. Living the Jesus way, trusting that He knows how to operate this life thing. Anger seems natural to us, and it is! But there's a way of handling it that Jesus offers and—surprise!—it's brilliant.

That's just one example, one way of applying what Jesus says and accepting His gift of peace. In the next chapter, we'll talk about still more ways.

We can lose sight of how wonderful it is, because there are so many religious clichés, and clichés lose their power. But make no mistake: joy is now available to the world. The Prince of Peace has come. And I love how Anne Lamott put it: "Peace is joy at rest, and joy is peace on its feet."[2]

On its feet! I like that.

Yes, life is hard, but God is good. And you know the rest.

TWENTY-FIVE

Speaking of Rest . . .
and Restrooms

The genius of being all about today.

This is going to be a great chapter, I think. This should wrap up the Nobel.

It's going to be about rest. But first, let's talk about stress, which, as you know, can hit you anytime, anywhere.

+

Often, I find myself feeling like I have no idea what is going on, like everyone else understands but I don't. In this case, I truly had no precedent for whatever was happening. It was a crowd of people, and I didn't understand what they were saying or doing. But they seemed happy. Maybe.

193

And one of them stepped forward to—obviously—hand me a pair of scissors.

Okay . . . ?

They turned me around, and my new friend, a young man named Ashwin, translated so I could understand what in the world was going on. "They want you to cut the ribbon!"

The crowd seemed very excited. I don't pick up on social cues quickly, but I realized this was an honor, for sure. I'm the ribbon cutter? Ashwin told me the crowd was honoring their guest, me, by allowing him to cut the ribbon for the new restrooms! It was a concrete-block building that sat next to a village in southern India. I was visiting with a small group from Compassion International, which had been part of the restroom project.

I didn't do anything to deserve this honor, but I accepted, and when I cut the ribbon, the crowd applauded wildly. We all smiled. I stood there for a little bit, not knowing what to do. It seemed like they were waiting for . . . me?

"Um . . . what's happening?"

Ashwin: "They want you to be the first to use it."

"Like . . . now?"

"Yeah, just go in and use it and come back out."

I was trying to talk to him in a hushed way without moving my lips for some reason, looking back and forth at everybody. I leaned my head in toward Ashwin.

"But I don't really . . . need to . . . *go* . . . so. . ." Ashwin nudged me forward.

I walked up a few steps in front of the crowd and ducked into the men's room. I figured I'd stand there for a minute and then come back out. I noticed the windows were up high, but it was open air. No glass. And I'm here to tell you that what I heard next filled me with dread: silence. The crowd outside was quiet. Waiting for me.

This was a pressure situation. I don't know how else to put it, except by typing a short sentence I hope never to type again: I didn't need to pee, but I *needed* to pee. I stood there in the heat and humidity and wondered how this kind of thing happens to me.

I will now end this story by telling you that, yes, it ended very successfully . . . and the movie rights are available for bidding. As I emerged back into the sunlight, the crowd applauded, like I'd just birdied the twelfth hole at Augusta.

✦

Anyway, I had a point with this: Stress comes at us a thousand ways. Some of it we bring on ourselves, I suppose. But then there are the unexpected India-restroom-christening scenarios in life. I'm sure you can relate.

And stress kills us. A great book to read on this is Robert Sapolsky's *Why Zebras Don't Get Ulcers*. He's a primate neuroendocrinologist who writes about how we humans are the only creatures who can actually worry about things that aren't threats. We can worry about what might happen tomorrow. Nobody else does that. We're special.

We're equipped with a fight-or-flight response to threats to help us survive. But it's only humans that can stay in that mode, and it does horrible things to our bodies and minds.

And then there's Jesus, telling us not to worry about tomorrow. Be like the animals. Don't worry. Worry doesn't help. "Each day has enough trouble of its own," He said (Matthew 6:34), and don't I know it.

> It's only humans that can stay in fight-or-flight mode, and it does horrible things to **our bodies and minds.**

I'm glad I've been busy writing a book on joy, because it's another built-in reminder for me to think about the goodness of God. We must be intentional to focus on His goodness because our culture seems precision-designed to make us worry, while offering nothing in the way of reassurance for our souls.

I had to remind myself just today of what I've been writing about in this book. I mentioned earlier that I've been booked (and this is not normal for me) for an interview on a network TV morning show, so my wife and I will need to fly to New York City next week. I haven't been stressed about it. But then I lay in bed this morning and thought, *Wait, what do I even wear? Will my head shaking be a problem? What if they put makeup on me?* and things like that. I could feel the stress, the shot of cortisol that would ensure I couldn't get back to sleep.

And then I remembered the stuff:

1. Be grateful. Specifically. Name specific things.
2. "Outsource" my worry. (*God, can You concern Yourself with that thing next week for me? If You've got it, I won't think about it.*)
3. Review Scripture in my mind, thinking about what's true and good again, like the writer of Lamentations.

> Yet this I call to mind
> and therefore I have hope:
> Because of the LORD's great love we are not consumed,
> for his compassions never fail.
> They are new every morning;
> great is your faithfulness. (3:21–23)

This writer managed to remind himself of this in the midst of deep anguish, seeing the complete destruction of Jerusalem by the Babylonians. I'm just going on a TV show.

It's amazing how we can do that. What *if* I look stupid on *GMA*? Well, I've looked stupid before. It'll just be another story to laugh about with friends (and probably include in my next book).

✦

Jesus did and said so many remarkable things. But this one in the Gospel of Matthew is . . . well, I can't describe how wonderfully unique this is:

> "Come to me, all you who are weary and burdened, and I will give you rest. Take my yoke upon you and learn from me, for I am gentle and humble in heart, and you will find rest for your souls. For my yoke is easy and my burden is light." (11:28–30)

This is God's message to us? "I'm offering rest. Partner with Me, and you'll find it."

For context, imagine ancient ideas of the gods. Would Zeus say this? No, Zeus would not say that. Zeus was a big jerk, which is why WWZD? bracelets have never taken off.

Jesus offers rest because the way of living that Jesus gives us is deeply restful.

We all live for something. This "yoke" talk is about taking the burden of whatever it is I'm living for and trading it in. His yoke is lighter, He said.

I can confirm this. I sometimes feel the pressure to have a Big Vision and accomplish some Big Thing or be More Significant and you know what? It's a *lot* of stress. Our culture loves Big Visions and Plans and Statements and so forth. But our culture is also acutely anxious and exhausted and angry.

But what if we just focus on the next thing? That's it. I've been trying this for some time now, based on what I've learned from studying how Jesus operated. So I want to be faithful with what and who crosses my path *today*. That's it.

Jesus told us to pray for our daily bread, the resources we need for today's challenges. The Big Picture and Other Big Capitalized Things? God can be trusted with those. That's His burden. Mine is much lighter now.

I really recommend it. It takes some unlearning because we have a society that worships "leadership." We have conferences and mountains of books about leadership. Everyone thinks they're supposed to aspire to be in authority. But Jesus, the One who knows how we flourish, told us to aspire to be a servant.

I can tell you that's why I'm writing this book. I'm not trying to write a big bestseller. I'm hoping that you're reading these words, flawed as they are, and that they add value to your life. Of course, we're all a mixed bag of motives. I'm also writing because I enjoy thinking about this stuff, the publisher gave me a deadline, and my family has grown fond of things like, say, groceries. So sure, that's in the mix.

But ultimately, when we see what the kingdom looks like, and we fall in love with that, we know that's what we want more than anything. Since it's not my kingdom, I'm not responsible for it. I just do my thing, today, and talk to God about it while I walk my dog.

> Tomorrow is tomorrow, and I have to trust that God is already there. He tells us He is.

Tomorrow is tomorrow, and I have to trust that God is already there. He tells us He is.

He's come to give me rest. I just have to work with Him. I just have to do my thing.

Stuff will happen today. Knowing me, probably weird stuff. Maybe another ceremonial ribbon cutting. I hope it's a bakery or something this time.

But whatever it is? Honestly, I'm not worried.

TWENTY-SIX

The Song You Will Sing

There's a strange scene in the Bible (and yes, there are a lot of strange scenes in the Bible) where a whole nation was singing, and then an old woman just started singing her own song.

It happened in Exodus, right after God parted the waters of the Sea of Reeds to allow His people to get away from Pharaoh and all his men. You probably know the story: God told Moses to raise his hand again, and the waters rushed in. The mighty Pharaoh and his army were suddenly no more. Not a single one of them survived.

Everyone was in awe, as you might imagine. They all started singing. It was long and triumphant and poetic, with lines like this: "Who is like you among the gods, O Lord—glorious in holiness, awesome in splendor, performing great wonders? You raised your right hand, and the earth swallowed our enemies" (15:11–12 NLT).

So there they were, all of them in unison, thanking God for what just happened. Their faith in Him had been vindicated! The song goes on for *eighteen* verses.

And then something happened that we barely notice in the grand sweep of all of these big events: a woman started her own song. It was Miriam the prophetess, Moses's big sister. She grabbed a tambourine and led the women in singing.

> Sing to the LORD,
> for he has triumphed gloriously;
> he has hurled both horse and rider
> into the sea. (v. 21 NLT)

I had never thought about this until I heard Rabbi David Fohrman talk about it. I'd never stopped and asked: Wait, *why* did she do her own song? And why is this even part of the story? Rabbi Fohrman said to look at all of this from her point of view.

This would be a great movie, actually—all from her point of view. Moses was eighty at this point. She was even older. So it would be like *Titanic* with the flashbacks from the memory bank of the old lady. I need to make this happen. I just need an awesome soundtrack and maybe $300 million.

We'd start with the lady singing, and then flash back to a misty morning many years earlier along a river. A young girl is there. She's very scared. She's standing still. She's watching something. And she's crying.

We see that she's watching a little basket, floating on the water among the reeds. Inside the basket is her little brother. He's just three months old. His mother and father didn't know what to do with him, because they are living as the slaves of a fearsome, genocidal ruler. He fears the growth of the Israelite population in his land, and he has a policy: all Israelite baby boys must be immediately drowned in the Nile.

The family tried hiding him. For months, they tried. But now they had no choice but a move of utter desperation: they were hoping somehow God would take care of him. The girl, Miriam, "stood at a distance to see what would happen to him" (Exodus 2:4).

It's hard to imagine things getting worse than that.

And then things got worse than that.

In modern times, imagine the genocidal ruler is, say, Adolf Hitler, and of all the people who could walk by at that moment . . . we see Hitler's own daughter. Now the story is over, right? Sure seems like it. Not only will the baby be drowned but the whole family may have to die as punishment.

But Pharaoh's daughter, the princess, opens the basket and feels sorry for the crying baby. Our hero girl, Miriam, makes a genius move: "Should I find a Hebrew woman to be the baby's nurse?" she asks the princess. The princess says yes, and even says she'll pay Miriam for helping.

Miriam walks home, carrying her little brother, Moses, back safely from the reeds. Can you imagine how she felt? What was she thinking then? *How did that just happen?!* is a fair guess.

You can read the rest of Moses's story, of course. About how he went on to become part of the tyrant's own household. How he killed an Egyptian man for beating an Israelite. How he went into hiding and spent decades in Nowheresville. And then how God decided it was time for Miriam's little brother to spring into action—as much as an eighty-year-old guy can "spring." We get the negotiations with Pharaoh, the plagues on Egypt, and then the ragtag nation of Israelites running for their lives, chased by an army of death.

Now we see them come to the water. More reeds. It's Pharaoh, coming for Moses after all. There's no way out of this, right?

But Moses tells the people, "Don't be afraid. *Just stand still and watch* the Lord rescue you today." (That's from Exodus 14:13 NLT, and I italicized that part because it precisely mirrors the language used to describe what Miriam was doing so many years earlier, standing and watching to see what would happen to her baby brother!)

And maybe our movie cuts to the other side of the sea, as the Israelites stand slack-jawed after watching Pharaoh and his unstoppable army be swallowed up. All of them gone. Again, I wonder what they were feeling and thinking. And again, *How did that just happen?!* is a fair guess.

So everybody starts singing and partying and dancing and thanking God. It's a natural reaction.

And when they're finished . . . Miriam remembers. She remembers that baby, those reeds, that river. All the fear. The hopelessness. Maybe wondering if the God of the Israelites cared at all or really was powerful enough to defeat the seemingly more successful gods of Egypt.

In the end, it wasn't her baby brother who drowned among the reeds. It was evil itself.

It would be hard for anyone else to fully understand.

So she starts her own song.

> In the end, it wasn't her baby brother who drowned among the reeds. It was evil itself.

She sings about the goodness of God. She couldn't have scripted all of this. Who could? She couldn't have seen any of this coming. Who could? And now she couldn't resist singing.

Knowing what she knew, and remembering what she remembered, who could?

If we could sit down for tea and conversation with old-lady Miriam, I wonder what worries we might have that we could talk to her about. Maybe we'd talk about worst-case scenarios for family or finance or just how messed up our country is or why the world feels so hopeless or whatever.

I have a feeling she'd be a patient listener, but I also suspect that every time we looked at her, we'd stop ourselves midsentence.

She'd have a certain look, I think; maybe a little pity mixed with bemusement, like she knows we really, truly don't need to be worried. Like we really could be at peace, and that we should have—you know—a sense of well-being, regardless of circumstances.

Like she knows how this all ends, and we need to know it, too, and we should really believe it.

So maybe I'd ask her to remind me: How does all of this end? I've seen some beautiful things, so much of the world. I've seen little kids get to run and play for the first time. I've seen moms cry tears of joy. I've seen my own kids grow up and become my friends. So much goodness.

But there's an ache to life. Even remembering all the stuff I went through as a kid—the trauma, fear, and heartbreak. So much pain in the world feels overwhelming if I stop to think about it. And terrible things can still happen to me, to us. How can any of this make sense? I can't get my head around it.

What was all of this about? How does this end?

And maybe she'd say, "Don't be afraid. Just *stand still and watch the Lord rescue you today.*"

And maybe we'd believe her.

Maybe we'd start believing we really are safe, after all. We'd wonder why we didn't see it all along, when Jesus told us we'd have troubles but to be of good cheer: *we could have been of good cheer all this time!*

Miriam had to sing her own song. She just had to.

I wonder what your song will be.

I wonder what mine will be too.

One thing I'm sure of: it'll be the motley lot of us, the formerly broken and seemingly hopeless; the formerly paralyzed, sick, and heartbroken; former strugglers and sinners and bumblers; all of us, together.

And we'll be dancing.

I can't wait. In fact, I'm starting now.

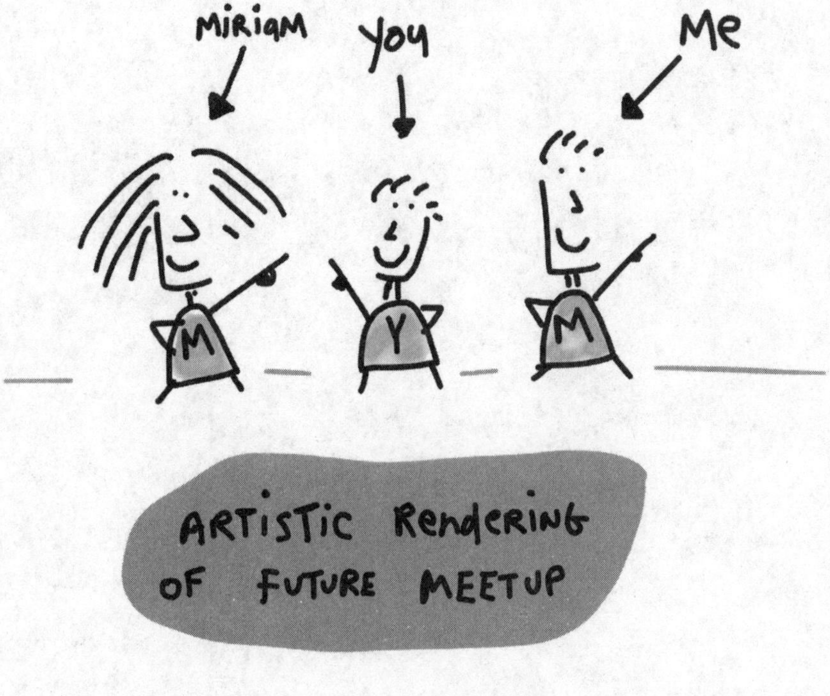

MIRIAM
YOU
ME
M
Y
M
ARTISTIC RENDERING OF FUTURE MEETUP

Acknowledgments

I want to thank my wife, Carolyn, without whom I'd . . . I don't know? I started a sentence I couldn't finish. She's part of who I am.

Thank you to Justice, Julia, Zach, and baby Scout. (Scout, when you can read this, please know that you contributed to the writing of this book by being the most delightful distraction imaginable.)

Thank you, Darin, as always.

Thank you to "Producer Sherri," Sherri Lynn, for being ever encouraging. And to her mom, Bev. You are both family.

Thank you to my insightful editors, Lauren Bridges and Kyle Olund, and the excellent W team at HCCP. Kyle, I want to thank you for being the artistic visionary who allowed me to include my inspiring stick-figure drawings.

Thank you to the people of CURE. All of you: nurses, housekeepers, moms and dads of the patients, donors, surgeons, techs, everybody. Especially, of course, all the boys and girls. Thank you for letting me be part of your stories. What an honor. And by the way, if you're reading this and want to see CURE in action: check out cure.org.

And thank *you* for reading the acknowledgments. I respect that. In fact, if I'm ever speaking in your area or something, or maybe we run into each other at the store or whatever, just say the words "I actually did read your acknowledgments," and I will scramble to find a prize. Maybe I'll pull out a coupon or a guitar pick or even Kohl's Cash if I have some. You deserve it.

Notes

Epigraph

1. John 16:33 NKJV; emphasis added.

Chapter 1

1. Dallas Willard, *The Allure of Gentleness: Defending the Faith in the Manner of Jesus* (San Francisco: HarperOne, 2016), 31.
2. C. S. Lewis, dedication to Lucy Barfield, in *The Lion, the Witch, and the Wardrobe* (Grand Rapids, MI: ZonderKidz, 2005).
3. Roger E. Olson, "Did Karl Barth Really Say 'Jesus Loves Me, This I Know . . . '?,'" Patheos, January 24, 2013, www.patheos.com/blogs/rogereolson/2013/01/did-karl-barth-really-say-jesus-loves-me-this-i-know.
4. Elizabeth Knowles, ed., *Oxford Dictionary of Quotations*, 7th ed. (Oxford University Press, 2009), 597.
5. "How Deadly Is Quicksand?," *Encyclopaedia Britannica*, www.britannica.com/story/how-deadly-is-quicksand.
6. Tim Mackie, "What Faith Is?," Tim Mackie Archives, August 14, 2017, YouTube video, https://www.youtube.com/watch?v=A-zK3Uy-QcY.

Chapter 3

1. Rob Bricken, "7 Moments in the Bible When Jesus Acted Very Un-Jesus-Like," Gizmodo, September 16, 2015, https://gizmodo.com/7-moments-in-the-bible-when-jesus-acted-very-un-jesus-l-1731054203.
2. Thomas Merton, *Thoughts in Solitude* (New York: Farrar, Straus and Giroux, 1999), 79.

Chapter 4

1. Dallas Willard, *The Divine Conspiracy: Rediscovering Our Hidden Life in God* (San Francisco: HarperOne, 1998), 66.
2. C. S. Lewis, *The Voyage of the Dawn Treader* (New York: HarperTrophy, 2000), 187.

Chapter 5

1. James Bryan Smith, *The Good and Beautiful Life: Putting on the Character of Christ* (Downers Grove, IL: InterVarsity Press, 2009), 179.

Chapter 8

1. "Conor McGregor Visits Wrigley Field," Chicago Cubs, November 5, 2021, YouTube video, www.youtube.com/watch?v=oWjoSWu-DkI.

Chapter 9

1. Thornton Wilder, *The Angel That Troubled the Waters* (1928), Library of America, accessed July 31, 2023, https://storyoftheweek.loa.org/2018/04/the-angel-that-troubled-waters.html.

Chapter 10

1. Candice Gaukel Andrews, "'Fernweh': A Farsickness or Longing for Unseen Places," Natural Habitat Adventures, May 8, 2018, www.nathab.com/blog/fernweh-a-farsickness-or-longing-for-unseen-places.

2. C. S. Lewis, *The Weight of Glory* (San Francisco: HarperOne, 2001), 30–31.

3. Eric Grundhauser, "Have You Ever Felt Homesick for a Place You've Never Been?," Atlas Obscura, February 27, 2018, www .atlasobscura.com/articles/homesick-for-place-you-have-never-been.

Chapter 11

1. G. K. Chesterton, *Orthodoxy* (Nashville: B&H Academic, 2022), 81.

2. Mike Yaconelli, "It's Time to Party," in *Fearfully and Wonderfully Weird: A Screwball Look at the Church and Other Things from the Pages of the Wittenburg Door*, ed. Doug Peterson and H. Winfield Tutte (Grand Rapids, MI: Zondervan, 1990), 166–67.

3. C. S. Lewis, *Letters to Malcolm* (San Francisco: HarperOne, 2017), 125.

Chapter 12

1. Frederick Buechner, "Wishful Thinking," in *Beyond Words: Daily Readings in the ABC's of Faith* (San Francisco: HarperOne, 2004), 130.

2. Eugene H. Peterson, *Traveling Light: Modern Meditations on St. Paul's Letter of Freedom* (Colorado Springs: Helmers and Howard, 1988), 57.

Chapter 13

1. Erika Edwards, "CDC Says Teen Girls Are Caught in an Extreme Wave of Sadness and Violence," NBC News, February 23, 2023, https://www.nbcnews.com/health/health-news/teen-mental-health -cdc-girls-sadness-violence-rcna69964.

2. Brennan Manning, *The Signature of Jesus* (Sisters, OR: Multnomah, 1996), 44–45.

Chapter 14

1. James Clear, "3–2–1: The Value of Reading One Good Book Per Year, and Lessons on Kindness and Generosity," *3–2–1 Newsletter*, June 15, 2023, https://jamesclear.com/3-2-1/june-15-2023.

2. Evan Easterling, "Oklahoma Softball Caps Banner Season with 3rd Straight Title," *New York Times*, June 9, 2023, www.nytimes.com /2023/06/09/sports/oklahoma-softball-national-championship .html.
3. "2023-06-06 WCWS Oklahoma Pregame Press Conference," NCAA Championships, June 6, 2023, YouTube video, www .youtube.com/watch?v=O2cT6uTHcCs&t=721s.
4. Elizabeth Barrett Browning, *Aurora Leigh: A Poem in Nine Books* (London: Chapman and Hall, 1857), 275.

Chapter 16

1. Barnabas Piper, "Behind the Song: Horatio Spafford & Philip Bliss, 'It Is Well with My Soul,'" *American Songwriter*, accessed July 31, 2023, www.americansongwriter.com/it-is-well-with-my -soul-behind-the-song-horatio-spafford-philip-bliss.
2. *Seinfeld*, season 3, episode 9, "The Nose Job," directed by Tom Cherones; written by Larry David, Jerry Seinfeld, Peter Mehlman; aired November 21, 1991.

Chapter 17

1. C. S. Lewis, *The Four Loves* (New York: HarperOne, 2017), 155–56.
2. Matthew Scully, *Dominion: The Power of Man, the Suffering of Animals, and the Call to Mercy* (New York: St. Martin's Griffin, 2002), 26.

Chapter 18

1. Suzana Herculano-Houzel, "The remarkable, yet not extraordinary, human brain as a scaled-up primate brain and its associated cost," *PNAS* 109, no. S1 (June 22, 2012):10661-10668, https://doi.org /10.1073/pnas.1201895109.
2. Ailsa Harvey and Elizabeth Howell, "How many stars are in the universe?," Space.com, February 11, 2022, www.space.com/26078 -how-many-stars-are-there.html.

3. Gary Reiner, "How Many Atoms Are in the Human Body?," *Who Knows Anyhow?* (blog), March 30, 2019, www.whoknowsanyhow .com/2019/03/30/how-many-atoms-are-in-the-human-body.

4. Richard Monson, "A Mustard Seed Has a Mass of About 0.002 Grams," Good Decisions, July 27, 2022, www.gooddecisions.com /a-mustard-seed-has-a-mass-of-about-0–002-grams.

Chapter 19

1. "Mark 1:1: The Beginning of the Good News and an Inscription About Caesar Augustus," *Read-Scripture* (blog), December 31, 2021, www.read-scripture.com/mark-1–1-and-priene-inscription; emphasis added.

Chapter 21

1. Leo Tolstoy, "June 11," in *A Calendar of Wisdom: Daily Thoughts to Nourish the Soul, Written and Selected from the World's Sacred Texts*, trans. Peter Sekirin (New York: Scribner, 1997), 175.

2. Brother Lawrence, *The Practice of the Presence of God, in Modern English*, trans. Marshall Davis (published by translator, 2013), 46.

Chapter 22

1. Brant Hansen, *Unoffendable*, rev. ed. (Nashville, TN: W Publishing, 2023), 42.

Chapter 23

1. "Generosity," BibleProject, November 25, 2021, Facebook video, 0:33, www.facebook.com/watch/?v=1079658942800661.

Chapter 24

1. Brant Hansen, *The Truth About Us* (Grand Rapids, MI: Baker Books, 2020), 10.

2. Anne Lamott, quoting her pastor, in *Some Assembly Required* (New York: Riverhead Books, 2012), 212.

About the Author

Brant Hansen ignited a nationwide conversation on anger and forgiveness with his first bestselling book, *Unoffendable*. His work has been featured by *Good Morning America*, *Focus on the Family*, the *Irish Times*, CNN.com, and others. He's a popular speaker known for his uniquely challenging, authentic, and humorous style. He's also host of the nationally syndicated radio show, *The Brant Hansen Show*, and cohost of the podcast *Brant and Sherri Oddcast*.

Brant was diagnosed with autism spectrum disorder and says he's thankful for it.

More about Brant can be found at branthansen.com, Brant Hansen Page on Facebook, and @branthansen on other social media.